The Wordsworth Book of
Urban Legend

The Wordsworth Book of URBAN LEGEND

RODNEY DALE

Foreword by
GEORGE MELLY

Illustrations by
BILL TIDY
Special guest
STEVEN APPLEBY

Wordsworth Reference

For customers interested in other titles from
Wordsworth Editions visit out website at
www.wordsworth-editions.com

For our latest list and a full mail-order service contact
Bibliophile Books, 5 Thomas Road, London E14 7BN

Tel: +44 0207 515 9222   Fax: +44 0207 538 4115
e-mail: orders@bibliophilebooks.com

First published 2005 by Wordsworth Editions Limited
8B East Street, Ware, Hertfordshire SG12 9HJ

ISBN 1 84022 303 0

Typeset by Antony Gray
Printed and bound in Great Britain by
Mackays of Chatham, Chatham, Kent

To
JUDITH
*without whose wifely support
and encouragement life
would be empty and meaningless*

Contents

Acknowledgements

Many thanks to George Melly for identifying the Whale Tumour Story in the days before it became the Urban Legend, and for penning the foreword and its update; to Bill Tidy for his ever-fresh illustrations; and to Steven Appleby for allowing me to reproduce the beeping graveyard.

Thank you Charlotte, Emma, Matthew and Zoë for helping to get it all together.

Many people in the last fifty or more years have said things which I have stored, 'photographically lined on the tablets of my mind'. Apart from members of my family, I have derived inspiration from: Stephen Adamson, David Attenborough, Mags & Rob Barrett-Jolley, Roger Barrington-Styles, John Bathurst, Jim Beebee, Roger Bennison, Peter Bill, Gill Booth, Allen Boothroyd, Mike Boursnell, Althea Braithwaite, Roger Briggs, David Brooke, Fred 'Titre' Brown, Rob & Liz Cameron, John Chilton, Marcus Clapham, Ray Clark, Dudley Clews, Billy Connolly, Christopher Cook, George Cooper, Hugo Davenport, Anne & David Davies, Len Douglas, Piers Dudgeon, Richard Duke, Chris Dunn, Bushy Eiloart, Tim Eiloart, Robert Erskine, Mike Everitt, Colin Fisher, John Forster, Elna Forsyth, John & Val Galpin, Antony Gray,* Joan Gray, Colin Haycraft, Mike Hoare, Anna Hodson, Adrian Horne, Andrew Houston, Donald Ingleton-Beer, Mick Jeffries, Gerry Johnson, Gina Keene. Chris Lakin, Hugh Lindeman, Maurice Lynn, Tommy Maddox, Michael Mansfield, Stanley Mansfield, Peter Manuel, Alan McCombie, Susie Messer, Janet & Jim Miller, Stuart Miller, Spike Milligan, Don Moss, Marjorie Mortimer, Roger Mottram, Peter Mullen, Hilary Muray, Michael & Valerie Grosvenor Myer, Laurence O'Toole, Keith Padbury, Mervyn Parry, Mike Payne, People at Parties, Robert Phillips, Roy Pitches, Deric Platt, Kitty Platt, Mark Platt, Carole Pook, Alex Popple, Barry & Steve Puttick,

* Antony reports that he knew UL tales as Swan's Leg stories before they were otherwise named; I would be interested to hear of other readers' descriptions. RD

Dave Reeve, Clive Reynard, Charles Rogers, Roger Rowland, George Sassoon, Sue Shimmels, John Shippey, Frank Sheridan, Tony Short, Clive Sinclair, Paul Smith, Shenton Smith, Bob Snodgrass, Christopher South, David Southward, Gerry Staite, John Stanford, Dick Stone, Alec Storr, Tracy Stoten, Strangers on Stations and in Trains, Bonnie Taylor-Blake, Pippa & Steve Temple, Ted Tetley, Rodney Tibbs, Tony Tidswell, Michael Till, Rosemary Vicary, Brigit & Hugo de Waal, Bill Walston, Sue Whitby, Ian Williamson, Gill Wills, John Wills, Ray Woodman and Harry & Joyce Wrightson.

I am also grateful to the following for permission to quote from their works: Russel Ash *Fact or Fiction?* Reader's Digest; Briggs and Tongue *Folktales of England* Routledge & Kegan Paul; *The Secret Life of Salvador Dali* Vision Press; Bergen Evans T*he Natural History of Nonsense* and *The Spoor of Spooks* Michael Joseph; Grundy *Punch* reproduced by permission of *Punch*; Hogg and Weeks *Military Small-arms of the Twentieth Century* (3rd edition) Arms and Armour Press; Lord Montagu of Beaulieu *The Gilt and the Gingerbread* Michael Joseph and Sphere Books; Eric Partridge *The Shaggy Dog Story*; Enid Porter *Cambridgeshire Customs and Folklore* Routledge & Kegan Paul; H Allen Smith *The Compleat Practical Joker* Arthur Barker; James Sutherland *The Oxford Book of Literary Anecdotes* Oxford University Press; Symons *Buller's Campaign* Cresset Press; E S Turner *The Phoney War* Michael Joseph.

Prologue

It was a perfect July evening in 1976; George Melly was to perform at the Guildhall, Cambridge, and we had met beforehand in the yard of the Eagle Tavern in Bene't Street.

George sat on a plastic beer-crate, wearing his Max Miller suit, with hat, cigar, cane and grin – exuding the charisma of a twentieth-century Samuel Johnson. Discussing some anecdote, he said: 'That's a whale-tumour story . . . Do you know what a whale-tumour story is?' At that time, I didn't. He continued:

> During the war, when whale-meat was offered as a substitute for beef, a woman bought some whale-meat steak, took it home, and put it on a plate before preparing it for the oven. Her husband was sitting in the living-room, and suddenly a movement in the kitchen caught his eye . . . on investigation, they found that it was the whale-meat, which contained a *live tumour*, gently throbbing . . .

A whale-tumour story is one of those that people swear is true – it happened to a friend of theirs, but you never actually meet this friend. And you keep hearing of the same thing happening to friends up and down the country . . .

After that, I started to notice and collect whale-tumour stories, and dredge further examples from my capacious memory. The first fruits of the labour, with some thoughts arising, were published as *The Tumour in the Whale* (Duckworth & W H Allen, 1978).

And in 1984, Duckworth published a further collection of tales – *It's true . . . it happened to a friend* – which carried on the work. By that time, the WTS had become the UL, or urban legend, by which title such tales are now dignified.

This book updates the original work, for there have been many new occurrences since 1978 – and attitudes have certainly changed since then. It does not purport to be a complete collection of tales to date, but it does explore many topics, both general and personal, that I hope will give some insights into ULs in particular and life in general.

I feared originally that writing about them might put a stop to the tales, since those who had read the book would give up telling them, and laugh at those told by people who *hadn't* read it – though, on balance, I thought this unlikely.

Persistent tellers would continue to assert that they knew the person to whom whatever it was happened and, finding the tale in the book, would use this as spurious evidence that it was indeed true – or perhaps that they were the person in the story. I have had to bear the attacks of those who were offended that I should dare to question what they knew to be true stories – having heard them so many times, perhaps.

But in their hearts of hearts they will know that, as before, they are unlikely to be challenged, even though the audience, having read the book, might not be quite as accepting as in the past.

There is a certain autobiographical leaning in my text, and many of the tales relate to the Cambridge in and around which I have lived for over sixty years, and to its University. I'm not apologising – just warning you, and telling you that I realise it.

Drawing on levels of authentication as in an auctioneer's catalogue, the stories I tell are of three types:

(a) 'I saw . . . ' or 'I did . . . ' mean exactly that – I am speaking from personal experience.

(b) 'A friend (or some named person) saw . . . ' means that, to the best of my knowledge and belief, what they said was true.

(c) 'A friend of a friend (foaf) saw . . . ' means that the tale has been reported from several quarters, that its provenance is shady, that it is almost certainly a UL.

You may ask why I include true stories. The answer, simply, is in the interest of truth, If I say here that something has happened to me, then you'll know that it's true. If you have heard that the same thing has happened to others, then either that's a coincidence, the likelihood of which you may judge from the story itself . . . or my experience has turned into a UL.

Certainly life does imitate art, and from time to time you will find that what was a UL is now a true story. Some examples appear in my commentary.

Or, of course, you may find me reporting as type (c) an incident which happened to you – in that case, you *are* the original, elusive foaf.

A Note on the Foaf

One of the first questions I was asked at the Sheffield conference (1982) was: 'Do you pronounce it "foaf" (to rhyme with "loaf") or "fo-af" (as in "he's so affable")?' I go for the former. I coined the word (well, it coined itself) in 1976 to short-cut having continually to say 'friend of a friend', the subject of so many urban legends. I had long been an aficionado of acronyms, and it was a bonus that 'foaf' has a certain clod-hopping cacophony. Since then, urban legends have become 'foaftales' (a sub-set of folktales), or even 'foafs' (friend-of-a-friend stories), and the newsletter of the International Society for Contemporary Legend Research is published as *Foaftale News*.

RODNEY DALE
Haddenham, Cambridgeshire
March 2005

Foreword

Materialising as I do in the very first paragraph of this book, I can hardly pretend to be surprised at its existence. There is, however, a deal of difference between an *idea* for a book, and its realisation, and here I can express nothing but admiration. That same fine July evening of which the author speaks may have contained the moment of its conception but, if Rodney Dale will allow me to change his sex (metaphorically), there is a world of difference between the few moments necessary to father a child, and the months of gestation and effort needed to bring it into the world.

The 'whale-tumour story' is part of the collective mythology of the bandwagon, a vehicle in which the John Chilton Feetwarmers and I spent so much of our middle-age. I think it was John himself who first, in reaction to some contemporary but equally unlikely tale, resurrected that moment of horror on the wartime dresser which is revealed in the opening pages of this book, but the rest of us had either heard and forgotten it or were able to produce similar instances of the need to believe the impossible and to attempt to insist on its veracity by citing its source. At all events it did little more than provide us with a convenient yardstick, and the source of a handy phrase to indicate scepticism. Nor would it have gone further if I had not happened to explain its meaning to Rodney Dale in that Cambridge inn-yard that fine summer evening.

Rodney has seen fit to describe me in flattering terms – to evoke both Dr Johnson *and* Max Miller in a single sentence is little short of fulsome. He chooses, however, to appear only as a witness, albeit a potentially constructive one. Here then are a few observations:

Rodney is one of those rare, enviable creatures who bridge, with no apparent strain, the Two Cultures as defined by C P Snow. On the one hand he has a knowledge of computers, science, mathematics and logic, and on the other a sense of fantasy and absurdity verging on the manic. Forced to choose a spiritual ancestor for him, I would propose Lewis Carroll. Dale's own grasp of logic indeed frequently leads him into a Wabe of Carrollian absurdity. He has a habit of pursuing an ill-considered statement with the obsessive air of the Bellman on the

track of the Snark. It is this quality which convinces me that this book
and its author were destined for each other, and to think of myself as
a mere catalyst.

Method and obsession are the horses that pull Rodney's mental
carriage. Dressed, for jazz functions at any rate, with near Bohemian
panache and a somewhat excessive fondness for shades of mauve,
sporting a well-behaved beard, he could be taken at first glance for a
'modern' painter in a *Punch* cartoon of the middle twenties. This
façade is however betrayed by his eyes which, while hiding behind his
glasses, comb reality like radar beams, registering instantly the passing
of whales with or without tumours. Here in this book are his findings,
methodical and dotty, and recorded with that crisp asperity that those
of us who know him will recognise as exactly his tone of voice.

There is no need for me here to pontificate on the need for absurd
mythology in modern man – Rodney Dale has himself performed that
task admirably, and happily in Bill Tidy (himself a formidable creator
of tripe-manufacturers and clog-dancers as insanely obsessional in
their beliefs as his subjects here) he has found the ideal illustrator.

Ahead of you is a museum of credulity. You will, of course,
recognise its absurdity – except in the case of just one or two stories
which you happen to know, irrefutably, and on excellent authority (a
friend of the wife's brother? a cousin of the man who mends the
washing machine?) are absolutely true . . .

GEORGE MELLY 1978

Twenty years on – no, over twenty-five years since I wrote that –
but whereas in many ways and none for the better (creaking knees,
forgetting people's names, having to get up four times in the night
etc) things have changed, this book has, if anything, gained in
authority and relevance – or at any rate appears to have done so.
The reason? Because, while Rodney was unaware of it at the time, it
was a pioneer effort, a seminal work, the rolling stone that started
an avalanche. Since its modest début, not only has it led to imitation
(at worst) and to amplification (at best); it has invaded Academe.
That whale tumour throbbing on the wartime dresser has spawned
university courses, conferences and seminars. Far from, as Rodney
feared at the time, killing off the credulity of those who believe in
the headless motorcyclist and his grizzly chums, people – while
admitting the absurdity of other tales in this genre – swear ever

more adamantly that the story they tell is true. It is this need to believe the impossible that hasn't withered under exposure, in fact if anything the ever-changing – and, for many of us, confusing – acceleration of the world around has made it more essential. 'I believe,' said Alice's White Queen, 'as many as six impossible things before breakfast.' Here, then, is Rodney's *ur-work*. He and I have eaten a lot of curries since 1978, but the book remains the crisply-written exposure of credulity it always was. Those who, for whatever reason – not having been born, for example – missed it first time round have a treat in store in this much augmented version.

GEORGE MELLY 2004

Introductory Survey

> It is necessary always to aim at being interesting rather
> than at being exact; for the spectator forgives everything
> except dreariness.   VOLTAIRE

In July 1982 I was invited to a 'meet the author' session at a
Conference – Perspectives on Contemporary Legend – run by the
University of Sheffield's Centre for English Cultural Tradition. I
was somewhat surprised to find that this gathering of the world's
eminent folklorists had heard of me, but when I got there I discovered that my book *The Tumour in the Whale* – even then almost
unobtainable – had become a standard work in the field of folklore.

My colleague on the platform was one of America's leading folklorists, Professor Jan (pronounced, appropriately enough, Yarn)
Harold Brunvand, who had recently published *The Vanishing Hitchhiker*, a collection of American 'urban legends'. I commend his
books to you.

In its time, *The Tumour in the Whale* gave rise to a remarkable display
of mass apathy, though some people – including the publisher – thought
that it was the title that put people off. However, it would appear to
have become essential reading for the professional collector of 'urban
legends', and that is why I am now revising and augmenting that seminal
work.

What is an urban legend? Ever since the dawn of time – before the
days of television even – man has felt the need to exercise God's
glorious gift of speech by talking to his fellows. Storytelling obviously
meets several needs: it fills silences on long winter evenings, it
preserves knowledge and traditions, and – by no means least – it
confers a special aura upon the teller: the camp-fire personality.

Some of the stories told are obviously funny (or supposedly
funny) – the joke and the shaggy dog story for example. Some are
not meant to be funny – folk tales and ghost stories, for example –
whose reception will vary according to the guise in which they are
served. If we are warned that we are about to hear a ghost story, our

minds may put themselves into that mode which suspends disbelief and makes the heart pump faster.

In some ways, the urban legend is the folk tale of the present, but it differs from the folk tale in that it is of paramount importance that the hearer should believe that it is true. This is why 'it is common practice for the artless teller to seek to impart that belief [in its truth] to his listeners by affecting kinship, or at least a lifelong intimacy, with the protagonist of the adventure related' (Alexander Woollcott).

Aficionados of the urban legend will immediately see that by its opening will ye know it: 'A strange thing happened to a friend of mine . . . ' These opening words, necessary to establish the truth of the story, in themselves sound warning bells that may mark it as untrue.

Another characteristic which ensures that the urban legend is not seen as a joke is its generally unpleasant or ghastly character – witness many examples in this book. This also gives those who seek such pleasures an almost legitimate means of referring to unpleasant or taboo subjects in otherwise polite company. Apparent seriousness of purpose is here essential to avoid ostracism.

To make sure that it is taken seriously, the urban legend must be credible, even if it is somewhat far-fetched; the manner of telling is such that probing the story is discouraged. When challenged, most amateur (by which I mean those who do not collect and write about them) tellers of urban legends seek strenuously to adduce further instant evidence that what they have said is true. This demonstrates what one might call the Pelion–Ossa syndrome – the more a tale is questioned, the more is its teller likely to sink ever more deeply into the quicksand of unjustified and unjustifiable defence.

There is, of course, another explanation for some urban legends. They can serve as awful warnings – don't put your poodle in the microwave oven Mrs Worthington, don't give lifts to little old ladies (they might have meat cleavers concealed in their handbags) and so on. To suggest to a child that it should not accept sweets from strange men merely gives rise to the question: 'Why?' To tell a story about someone who accepted sweets from strange men with some gruesome consequence, may seem somewhat macabre – and possibly contrary to this month's notions of child rearing – but it will certainly answer any questions before they are asked.

The existence of the UL – though not under that banner – has been recognised, but its characteristics were not, I think, properly explored in public until the publication of *The Tumour in the Whale*. In 1969, Richard M Dorson wrote:

> The joke, the shaggy dog, the tall tale, the numbskull story abound among educated city folk and deserve acceptance in the corpus of folktales. Little attempt has yet been made to gather and examine these forms although Eric Partridge did devote a book to the Shaggy Dog Story . . . . The humorous, modern story lore belongs not to regions but to mobile society and easily crosses the Atlantic between England and America. Macabre legends also thrive in the modern metropolis. The newly uncovered modern legend of 'The Stolen Corpse' [page 60] was first reported in England in 1963, and within the year it had been recorded in the US.

That is obviously a start, though the UL is by no means confined to 'educated city folk' – Dorson seems to have some stereotype in mind – and there is confusion between the 'humorous story' and the 'macabre legend'.

Collectors such as Briggs, Emrich, and Stith Thompson have recognised what we would call ULs, but had no common name for them. In their detailed analyses of legend, the UL, the myth of today, seems to have fallen by the wayside. Having said that, it would be fair to ask how one recognises a UL anyway. One way is to become familiar with the genre, by reading this book, for example. But first, let us have a look at some classes of story, which will help us to put the UL into context.

The joke is presented with the idea of making the hearer laugh. Sometimes, a presenter is clearly out to achieve this – indeed he may be billed as 'the world's funniest man' (what a title to live up to, although '*arguably* the world's funniest man' reeks of faint praise), he may be introduced as a comedian, he may draw a cartoon or comic strip. All these are signals which warn the audience: 'my intention is to make you laugh'. Sometimes the material is presented deadpan, and the presenter does not mind (ostensibly at least) whether or not the audience laughs. The larger the audience, the more likely is someone to catch on sooner rather than later; if the audience is one person, the deadpan joke is a leg-pull.

Jokes come in all shapes and sizes. Consider Groucho Marx's elegant:

> What? *Spring* in the air and *fall* in the lake?

or the multi-pun line:

> I call my mate Nagasaki, because he's both – unlike Kurt Weill, who was neither.*

or the entomological:

> When the zoology prof asked the student where he had been the previous day, he replied that he had been out in the field, studying *Phyllostomus grylloides.*†

At the sorting-office, they open all the mail addressed to Father Christmas, and one year found one from an old-age pensioner (sorry, senior citizen) living alone, who asked for five pounds so that he could give himself a Christmas treat. The supervisor was very touched by this letter, and pinned it up on the canteen notice-board, with a box beneath it for contributions. When he counted the money, it came to £3.72, so he made it up to four pounds by donating the difference, and sent it off to the old man, 'with the compliments of Santa Claus'. The next day, there was a note from the old man: 'Dear Santa, thank you very much for the money – but I reckon those thieving gits at the Post Office must have nicked a quid'.

There's the humour of pathos, laughter equals tears, the clown wanting to play Hamlet – though if he ever did, we're not told who won.

Each nation has an associated one about whom it tells jokes. Jugoslavs tell Lala jokes, Germans tell Scottish jokes (as a surrogate for telling Jewish jokes?) the Danes tell Aahrus jokes, Canadians tell Newfie jokes and the English tell Irish jokes.

That such pairings, and the need for such pairings, exist may be a clue to the impossibility of a successful European Union. The land-mass of Europe has had centuries to integrate itself into one people with a common language and a common currency. And has it done so? No. Why not? It seems clear that national identity is so powerfully to be preserved that there is no hope of integration. Even on our little

---

* For those who need an explanation, my mate is both a nagger, and sarky; while Weill was neither curt, nor vile.
† The cricket bat.

island the English, the Scots and the Welsh have remained as separate nations, even to the extent of their seeking to set up their own governing bodies, an act which flies in the face of integration. The North East seems to have had the right idea in voting not to dilute its government, though there do appear to be unelected Regional Assemblies creeping in through the back door, as it were.

Most people want to 'belong' – to their families, their immediate communities (which may be the street, the housing estate, village &c) and so on in larger and larger areas as seen in 'This book belongs to . . . England, UK, Europe, The World, The Solar System, The Galaxy, The Universe'. The level at which belonging has any real meaning diminishes as the list progresses.

So the most important level of government must be the Parish Council, since it surely understands local needs better than any other body, followed by the District Council and the County Council, ever more remote from the 'grass roots'. Yet the more remote the body, the more power it yields. There is an argument that this is back to front, and if we look at the whole system logically, it becomes obvious – I submit – that the political integration of Europe (or any other collection of countries) is a non-starter and we should never have got anywhere near the present well-nigh inextricable position. When the first language of all nations is Esperanto, or Volapuk (or, better still, English!) it may be time to start considering some sort of integration. Until then, stop wasting everybody's time and money. Free trade doesn't need all this fancy dress. The myth of political union may be the biggest UL of all.

Back to the Irish jokes. Many of these are one-liners, and concern such topics as the Irishman who bought a black and white dog because he thought that the licence would be cheaper (an observation rendered obsolete by the abolition of the dog licence). Or who, on seeing a lorry-load of turf pass by, remarked wistfully that he'd like to be able to afford to send his lawn away to be cut.*

Be that as it may, the Irish do have an endearing logic of their own, and I will illustrate this with a true story. There is an Irish builder called Frank on whose expertise I call from time to time. I was having some trouble with leaking gutters, so I asked Frank if he could come

---

* And when it's returned for relaying, you can always spot the Irish turf-layers by the foreman's periodic exhortation: 'Green side up; green side up'.

along with his longest ladder, for at that time we lived in a three-storey house. He arrived, and I asked him how long his ladder was.

'Twenty-five feet, if it's fully extended, but unfortunately you can't fully extend it.'

'Oh, why's that?'

'It's broken.'

However, he was able to get on to the roof, and found two problems – the gutters were full of tennis balls (easily remedied), and the lead was split (not so easy).

'It's a plumber's job – I'll have to get George in, he's a plumber. You know George – he delivers your milk.'

'Oh, yes.'

However, the removal of the tennis balls made a great improvement, and it was only when I thought that a little preventive maintenance wouldn't come amiss that I called Frank again.

'Oh, yes. We need George. Tell you what, I'll see if he can come out with me on Saturday morning.'

Apparently he could, for we were awoken by the scraping of ladder on wall on Saturday morning. I kept out of the way, not wishing to hold up the proceedings. However, at the appropriate hour I went out to offer refreshments, and was surprised to find George the plumber holding the ladder, and Frank on the roof doing the job. When they'd finished, I asked Frank why he'd needed a plumber to hold the ladder if he was going to do the job himself.

The explanation seemed perfectly logical:

'Well, you see, George can't stand heights.'

Irish stories are not a new phenomenon. In his autobiography at the turn of the last century (1901), the cartoonist and illustrator Harry Furniss tells of 'a story going the rounds' wherein some Irish builders had been instructed to build a wall round a ruined church to protect it. To save materials, they drew on the fabric of the ruined church.

The practical joke is a perfectly-defined genre which some, nevertheless, seek to ignore, though they will readily admit to the existence of 'pranks' which, when examined, turn out to be practical jokes. H Allen Smith's monograph on the subject was published half a century ago; it is, however, an important authority and sourcebook for many stories which have turned up in other guises since it was written – some as ULs.

In 1965, John Forster advertised himself in the *Mensa Bulletin* as he was seeking a job as an accountant: Cambridge Consultants, needing one and naturally drawn towards anyone advertising himself in *MB*, took him on. John started on 8 March, and on 1 April we received a letter from the Floral Research Association seeking our advice on preserving cut flowers, to fight 'the ever-increasing competition from the "plastic" flower market.' We replied to the FRA that we would be delighted to be engaged on this fascinating problem, but heard no more. John hadn't wasted much time; we found later that the 'FRA' happened to be at his parents' address.

Later that year another colleague, Althea Braithwaite, who had just started to manage my printing company, received a charming letter purporting to come from the Vicar of Swaffham Prior and thanking her in advance for her generous donation to his repair fund. This worried Althea, but we worked out that the letter must have been sent by John, who had found a record of her visit to the church in the visitors' book.

Now, the reason that he had visited Swaffham Prior was that he collects postmarks. It was, therefore, natural that he should have noticed that some of his letters (for some irrelevant reason which never came to light) were travelling all round Will's mother's before they were delivered to him. This story got into the papers. And that was our chance.

We printed a one-off letterhead for the 'Union of Post Office Operatives' and wrote John a letter from the 'Convening Shop Steward' saying that if he didn't retract his vile imputations of Post Office inefficiency, the whole of the Post Office would come out on strike. John arrived at work the following day looking distinctly ill.

Our preparations had been thorough; the type had been set for the letterhead, and distributed immediately afterwards. The materials used for make-ready had been taken home and burnt. But we had made one mistake. The piece of paper on which we had printed the letterhead was a sample sheet, and had a note of its provenance printed on the bottom – this we had cut off and put in the dustbin. John went through several inky dustbins that evening, looking for evidence – and found this narrow, matching strip of paper. He deserved to.

A practical joke can become a UL quite easily. The following may be correctly ascribed, but when one hears it told of, for example, a member of the French resistance in a train with two large German ladies, one becomes suspicious.

Lord Halifax, formerly Ambassador to the United States, was travelling to Bath in a railway compartment, also occupied by two very prim middle-aged ladies who were strangers to each other. The train entered a tunnel and the compartment was engulfed in darkness. Lord Halifax placed the back of his hand to his mouth and kissed it noisily several times. When the train reached the station he arose, doffed his hat, and said: 'To which of you charming ladies am I indebted for the delightful incident in the tunnel?' He left them glaring hatefully at each other.

The shaggy dog story is a species of deadpan joke which rambles on and on, and may reach its punchline before the fact that it is meant to be funny is detected. By some coincidence, it is some fifty years for the shaggy dog story, as it is for the practical joke, since a monograph on the subject appeared, compiled by the indefatigable Eric Partridge. It is a valuable work of identification, but our familiarity with the genre has mellowed since 1953, and we are better able to see a shaggy dog coming when it does.

At a 'local' in one of London's suburbs – so far as that goes, it might equally well have been in Paris or a New York suburb – a regular, of twenty years' moderate drinking, entered a new phase of enjoyment when a stranger began to frequent the bar. Not that he was interested in the stranger but in the dog that always accompanied him and did so much to enliven the evening.

The first time the stranger and his dog came into the room, which, in an older tradition fast dying out, possessed rather a good piano, the man ordered a pint o' bitter, sat down on a stool, patted the dog's head, and quietly urged him to 'play something for us, Smoky. Something lively. This dump's like a morgue, we must do something about it.'

To the amazement of the regulars and the preparing-to-be-resentful barman, the dog sedately walked to the piano and adjusted the stool. Without looking round for preliminary applause, nor in fact receiving any, it started to play a very catchy thing from the most popular musical comedy of the moment. The animal played very well, without any irritating mannerisms or large, pretentious gestures. On being asked to 'play us another, do!' and seeing that this was not mere politeness but genuine appreciation, the modest executant played two other numbers from the same musical.

For many evenings this sort of thing continued. The regulars would ask, now for 'Nelly Dean' or some other sentimental ballad, now for a specifically Cockney song, such as 'My Old Dutch', and occasionally for a more classical piece. One night, whilst everyone was listening raptly to a most artistic rendering of Handel's 'Largo', a famous music-hall manager strolled in to quench a raging thirst. Suddenly the visitor realised that, whoever was playing, he certainly 'knew his stuff'. He was amazed to see that it was a dog, a very ordinary looking dog. 'Surely not,' he muttered to himself, 'it's far too early for that.'

'Plays well, don't you think?' remarked the dog's owner.

'He sure does. Would he play *The Warsaw Concerto*?'

'Piece of cake. Hey there, play *The Warsaw* for the gentlemen, will you? And don't pull your punches.'

The dog played this spectacular piece with spectacular virtuosity. 'Anything else you'd like?'

'Yes, Liszt's *Hungarian Rhapsody* – that very fast, difficult one all the most florid pianists love to play – and so seldom can.' (That'll fox him, he thought; this bloke won't know the meaning of 'florid' . . . not at all sure I do myself; anyway, the dog'll never have heard of Liszt, but if I'm wrong, it'll prove that the creature's good, so good that I'll sign him up.)

The 'canine pianist' – already the astute music-hall manager was composing an advertisement – had no trouble in dealing with this example of musical pyrotechnics. Bewildered, the manager, not because he wished to know but simply because he hated to give himself away to these simpletons of the suburbs, blurted:

'Yes, the dog is good; in fact, marvellous.' Pause – 'By the way, can the animal orchestrate?'

'Orchestrate? Don't be silly! Haven't you noticed that my dog is a bitch?'

And Partridge adds a footnote:

That, more or less, is how the story is usually told; that, exactly, is the wording of the owner's final speech. By the majority, the story is thought to stand very satisfactorily on its external merits. It does. By the Greek scholar and by the etymologist, however, the conclusion is enjoyed for another reason.

Quite.

The ghost story may be told for various reasons – to exemplify the existence of the supernatural, to challenge the hearer's credulity, to make the flesh creep, or just to entertain, just as the billing 'the world's funniest man' is not calculated to help the billee, so does the ghost story find it increasingly difficult to live up to any promise of 'spine-chilling eeriness', *etc.* The ghost story shares with the UL the characteristic that, if there is any laughter in it, it is secondary to the theme: the laughter in no way detracts from the 'truth of the story, or turns it into a joke.'

Many of the colleges of Cambridge are allegedly haunted; the following tale belongs to Jesus College:

A Roundhead parson called Byfield was billeted in Jesus College during the Civil War. Cromwell's soldiers had little respect for learning and most of the scholars had fled the college rather than brave their jeers and taunts. One of the few to remain, a Fellow named Allen, had the room above Byfield's and night after night the ignorant and superstitious Roundhead heard him chanting his strange formulae, convinced he was communing with his Master, the Devil. After a while, Byfield realised he no longer heard Allen's heavy human footsteps leaving the room at night and stumbling down the stair in the dark, but only a quick, light pattering. One night, unable to stand the suspense any longer, Byfield tentatively opened the door to see a huge black cat trot past. Trembling with his own daring, he crept up the stairs to Allen's room which was empty . . . save for a few papers covered with mysterious and evil signs.

Night after night Byfield lay in bed listening to the inhuman footsteps pattering past his door at midnight and returning stealthily at dawn. One by one, soldiers billeted in the college died. One night, Byfield could stand no more. He crept out of his door and took a large horse-pistol from the rack outside the nearby armoury. He waited for the cat and, when he saw it, fired full in its chest. With an unearthly scream the animal disappeared into the night, and Byfield returned to his room convinced that God's will had been done. Next morning Allen's body was discovered in a grove of trees by King's Ditch, where the troopers went to draw water for their horses. A great horse-pistol bullet had torn a hole through his chest and a trail of blood, thick gouts of it, led from the armoury by the foot of the stair to the grove where the body lay. Suicide. That was the verdict. The necromancer, unable to bear the weight of his own evil, had shot himself in his room and dragged himself outside to die under the stars with which he had kept his unholy communion. That night, the body was laid out in Allen's customary room, above Byfield's bed. Byfield was gripped with horror as he lay in the paralysing silence. Desperately, he prayed for forgiveness and, as he finished, heard the door of the room above open and soft, pattering footsteps descend the stairs. He steeled himself to go to Allen's room: empty. No dead man with shot-mangled chest and staring eyes lay on the bed. Then he heard it: soft, furry footsteps, stalking him. He swung round to see the cat, eyes ablaze, poised to spring. 'Oh my God, make haste for my help,' gabbled Byfield, sinking down beside the empty bed. His hands closed on the stiff corpse of Thomas Allen, where he was discovered the next morning, raving. He died within the year.

Many ghost stories are incredibly wenge – that is to say, both the teller and the listener begin to glaze and lose interest before the end; or the end, when it arrives, makes them wish that they hadn't started.

As an example of a wenge ghost story, I would quote that of a London theatre, which 'was reputed to harbour the ghost of an irritable ex-Thespian in astrakhan collar that used to be seen in the vicinity of the manager's office.' The manager said that he had no doubt that the place was haunted, though he had never seen the ghost himself, but had talked to other people who thought that they might have done. (Is that it? Yes.)

Folk tales very often turn out to be wenge as well – not that I'm knocking the collectors and classifiers of folk tales you understand; I'm just pointing out that, out of context, folk tales are sometimes not very tellable.

The Good Magpie – There was once a gentleman who used to ride on horseback every day. One day he had occasion to call at a house by the roadside, where a woman and her little boy lived. While he was talking to the woman, he saw that she was making the oven hot, and the little boy said to him, 'Mother's holing the oven to put me in.'

But the gentleman thought the boy was only joking, so he took no heed and rode away. But he had not gone far before a magpie crossed his path, and kept flying in front of his horse, and would not go away. So at last he thought that the magpie wanted him to turn back. So he rode straight back to the house, and when he got there he found that the woman had gone and that the poor little boy was roasting in the oven.

The Man Who Got Into His Cart – One May I met and stopped to talk to an elderly carter in a Quantock Lane. After mutual admiration of the hill pony I rode, and of his solid Shire mare, we went on to discuss their ways. Yes, they had both been difficult that day, and so, all unasked for, out came this tale: ' 'Tis May, you see,' said the carter. '*Always troublesome they are then*. I don't never trust'n, not even the old 'oss yur. I've worked she twenty years tew. My wife she have an old uncle over to they Blackdowns and they were carting stones to *mend their Church*. Uphill 'tis and a nasty piece of road – they was those days, all stones – and there was a bit of a bank down over. I'd awalk any 'oss up there and down over but there was a carter, he did get intew the cart see – and *summat* gave his 'osses a fright and he was killed outright. In May 'twas. There's a verse over at the church there. No; I don't like May. Never tell what a 'oss will take and do.'

The old wives' tale – or folk belief may be in one of two sharply-defined categories: either it contains some truth or it doesn't. With the current trend towards mysticism and debunking of science, many old wives' tales are being got out and polished in an attempt to show that our ancestors 'knew a thing or two', or 'weren't stupid'. Of the sort which we may surely discount is the belief that worms cause toothache:

> If a worm eat the tooth, take acorn meal and henbane seed and wax, of all equally much, mingle these together, work into a wax candle and burn it, let it reek into the mouth, put a black cloth under, then will the worms fall out.

Or again:

> An approved remedy for a wolfe in a womans brest. Take crabbs when they be thorough ripe roste ym and when ya be thorough rosted spread ym on a cloth and lukewarme lay ym unto the sore brest and it will help the woman greined it must be drest twice a

day and when you pull of the plaster snatch it of hastily and perhaps ye shall see ye worm come forth or appear yn if you can take hold of it pull it out if you may be suffered.

On the other hand, there are those tales with more substance – such as that chewing willow bark (*Salix* sp) cures headaches – for has not the tree given its name to the salicylic acid which it contains, and is this not the principle of aspirin (rediscovered by Revd Edward Stone of Chipping Norton in the 18th century)?

Popular fallacies are an extension of old wives' tales, and begin to take us away from our subject of interest, for many popular fallacies are beliefs which are never articulated. If, however, they are brought into conversation, they nearly always have some foaf to support them – someone whose hair turned white overnight, or who has seen the Indian rope trick. People do not like their pet beliefs challenged.

Essential for students of popular fallacies are Ackermann, Evans, and Ward though the first, dating from 1924, contains many 'popular fallacies' which one hardly recognises as such today:

'That a Ventriloquist Talks in his Stomach – The etymology of this word has a great deal to answer for, as it no doubt keeps the popular idea alive. Certain animals, to wit the lobster and the crayfish, have teeth in their stomachs;* but, as far as we know, they do not possess the power of producing audible sound by means of those organs.

---

* gastroliths, actually

'On this subject, Prof Huxley, FRS, says: 'What is called *ventriloquism* (speaking from the belly), and is not uncommonly ascribed to a mysterious power of producing voice somewhere else than in the larynx, depends entirely upon the accuracy with which the performer can simulate sounds of a particular character, and upon the skill with which he can suggest a belief in the existence of the causes of these sounds . . .'

The Revd Dr Brewer also provides good value in explaining the world around us:

'Q *Why is not* old beer *and* strong porter *made* sour *by lightning*?
A   Because the *fermentation is more complete*; and, therefore, is less affected by electrical influence.
Q   *Show the wisdom of God in making air* a bad *conductor*.
A   If air were a *good conductor* (like iron and stone) heat would be drawn *so rapidly* from our body, that we should be *chilled to death*.'

Really popular fallacies, such as the superiority of brown eggs over white eggs, may never die. Often, they are harmless enough, save that, as Goethe said: 'Nothing is more harmful to a new truth than an old error.'

Popular fallacies may easily become ULs. Enid Porter writes:

Generations of men have been informed that MAs and Doctors may play marbles on the steps of the Senate House [Cambridge] on Degree Days, and that anyone wearing Lincoln Green has the indisputable right to practise archery in Petty Cury. So long in fact have these two fictions been maintained that they are now almost believed as based on historical fact.

I remember hearing that, according to a University Statute dating from the time of Richard II – or some other suitably remote monarch – it was indeed an indisputable right to practise archery in Petty Cury. The story went – and I heard it several times – that some undergraduates had discovered this right and then, with the appropriate equipment and clothes, had proceeded to hold up the traffic in Petty Cury (then a carriageway) while they exercised it. The story sometimes concluded that it had been necessary to repeal the right by Act of Parliament, or sometimes that the Proctors had dredged up some retaliatory Statute requiring the archers to perform some penance – such as coughing up 6/8*d*.

A similar belief, which I have again heard from many sources, is that one is allowed to relieve oneself against the rear nearside wheel of a horsedrawn vehicle. The story continued that this law was held, in the High Court, to allow a motorist to use the wheel of his vehicle for the same purpose. Or, variantly, he is 'got' on the point of law that he was using the wrong wheel.

One is put in mind of the rural interpreter of the Railway Terms & Conditions (according to *Punch* 1869):

> Cats is 'dogs' and rabbits is 'dogs' and so's Parrats, but this 'ere 'Tortis' is a insect, and there ain't no charge for it.

A story still current, and on the same theme, concerns the change from horse to motor-cabs. Plying for hire is hedged about with rules, and in the old days cab-drivers had to carry a bale of hay for the horse. This provision was not withdrawn as cabs became motorised and a taxi-driver found himself in court for failing to provide the statutory bale of hay for the non-existent horse.

The Royal Artillery changed from horses to motors as well, and a time-and-motion man was worried to find that one of the gun-crew had nothing to do. Research revealed that, in days of yore, the now unemployed man was the one who had held the horse.

Some pearls of received wisdom are so widely known that an author would be thought lax were he not to mention them where a mention would be expected. For example, writers on the early history of jazz just *have* to mention the wax cylinder recording of the music of the pioneer cornettist Charles 'Buddy' Bolden (1877–1931) that is so rare that its existence has never been proved. And writers on Lord (Michael) Heseltine would be thought lacking in knowledge if they omitted to mention the strenuously denied back of an envelope on which he was supposed, at Oxford, to have mapped out his career (Fifties: millionaire. Sixties: MP. Seventies: Minister. Eighties: Cabinet. Nineties: Downing Street.)

The urban legend (or whale-tumour story) is the subject of our book, and contains many elements from the above genres. One of its most important characteristics, however, is that the teller should be believed; for that reason he claims personal involvement with the protagonist, an almost certain talisman for securing invulnerability.

To make sure that the story is not seen as a joke, it is often unpleasant or ghastly, as witness many of the examples in this book.

To make sure that it is taken seriously it is credible, even if somewhat far-fetched; the manner of telling is such that probing the story is discouraged, as we have seen.

It may also be topical – which at once makes it suspect. When the film *Jaws* came out (1978), for example, I began to hear of a foaf surfing when: 'Crunch!' a shark takes a bite out of his 'solid fibreglass surfboard'. After a time, I heard of incidents of the shark slicing the surfboard in half – longitudinally – with its dorsal fin.*

Since timeliness can play an important part in the fashioning of a UL, it is not unusual to find the ULs of yesterday becoming the jokes of today, as understanding spreads. My old Granny used to tell this tale: at the time when the electrical telegraph was striding across the country, one old couple in particular observed the activities of the linesmen and took a keen interest in the idea that the wires could be used to transmit messages. So at Christmas they bought a pair of boots for their son who was in the big city, fastened his address and a seasonal message to them, climbed up a ladder, and hung them on the

---

* Now, once again, life imitates art as recounted in her book by surfing *manchote* Bethany Hamilton.

telegraph pole outside their cottage. They were delighted the next day to find the boots gone and a message fastened to the pole: 'Dear Mum and Dad, thanks for the boots, just what I wanted, Merry Christmas to you both, love Jack.'

Since I was very young at the time and needed to know more about this, Granny explained that it was an old tramp (presumably also equipped with a ladder?) who had taken the boots and left the note. I felt very glad for that old tramp.

The telegraph came to the notice of the public in 1845, when one John Tawell murdered a woman named Hart at Salthill, and fled by the Great Western Railway from Slough to London. As he looked out of the carriage window, little did he know that his description was being flashed along those dipping telegraph wires; when he arrived in London he was arrested and, in due time, tried, found guilty, and hanged. Some time later, a group of strangers was travelling in silence on the same route when one of them pointed to the telegraph wires and exclaimed in awe: 'Them's the cords that hung John Tawell'.

As I have said, the UL has to be distinguished from a joke whose purpose is to amuse the listener and, for this reason, its core has to be anything but funny, and is often downright unpleasant. I say 'the core' because there are certainly many which do raise a laugh, but whenever this happens, it does not detract from the apparent truth of the story.

Often, the humour of the UL is the humour of relief. My Grandfather told of an incident (incident – there's a word for you) in the trenches in the First World War when a brother officer clambered up in the wrong place at the wrong time and was cut in half with a burst of enemy machine-gun fire. His top half fell down, and the legs remained standing for a time before they, too, toppled over. Grandfather's reaction was to laugh.

This is nothing like the laughter of humour, however. It is compounded of . . . Horror? Relief that it didn't happen to you? And if you *didn't* laugh, what *would* you do?

Serendipity has always played an important part in my research, and when I first wrote the above words (1976), I immediately came across a passage in *Radio Times*, an account by Stanley Reynolds of his hearing, as a young infantryman in Texas, a black prison-gang singing a work song:

> The scene, the beauty of their singing, of these black men who were the grandsons or great grandsons of kidnapped African men and women, the still slave descendants of slaves, burned our eyes. Someone would have to make a joke, or it would not be bearable.

So does Bottom say (*MND* III.i):

> I will walk up and down here, and I will sing, that they shall hear that I am not afraid.

It is whistling in the dark.

We can share our tears as we can share our laughter. When someone dies we can reduce our grief by sharing it – there is an indescribably pleasurable pain in breaking the news to others. Perhaps, by being the bearers of sad tidings, we are gaining attention for ourselves and taking our minds off the source of grief. Certainly there is some element of reflected glory in telling some anecdote of the deceased – *de mortuis nil nisi bonum*, and the banal and the trivial assume an inflated importance until our memory of the departed comes into perspective, and the anecdotes sink back into their triviality. There is no doubt that people closely connected with bad news tend to share it with anyone at hand, including those who have little interest* – and that equally those less closely connected with it may tighten their assumed connections.

While on the subject of sharing grief, it is worth pointing out that in the world of the movies, the weepie (not to mention the horror) has as strong a place as the comic.

If you care to think on, you might wonder why, if the X-film is denounced as likely to incite violence and to deprave, the comic film is not denounced as likely to incite people to treat the serious business of life with levity, and to bring into question the gravity of the church, the law, the civil service, parliament and so on. If you think that the vulgar literature, sports and pastimes of today are likely to deprave, corrupt and incite violence, take a look at those of yesteryear.

When Vic Matthews took over Beaverbrook Newspapers, and stated that he 'wanted to talk about the good things that are being done', I remembered the newspaper in the US that printed only good news. It went out of business – so which will go first, the policy or the papers? People like bad news, and it travels faster than good – how soon after the event did *you* hear of the assassination of JFK? Or of 9/11? When I first heard something garbled about the twin towers, my mind flew to Wembley Stadium.

Marketing creates the conditions in which sales can take place. There is surely little doubt that violence begets violence, just as litter begets litter – if whatever it is is all around you, you give little thought to making your own contribution to it. The 'marketing' is the apparent acceptability of whatever it is in the environment; the 'sales' is your becoming seduced into taking part in it.

There are also degrees of violence. Is it true and, if it is, is it a coincidence, that as swearing has become more commonplace, stabbings and other violence have increased? If you have words reserved for 'those difficult occasions', they provide whatever

---

* We call this a 'head-dropper – the only possible reaction to statements such as: 'my mother's dog has just died'. The problem of what expression to adopt rears its head again when one is faced, for example, with someone singing impromptu, *a capella*, and badly.

aggression you need. But when your entire vocabulary is in everyday use, you have to move on to the next tread of the stair ('escalation'). Here's yet another initiative for the Home Secretary: 'Hand in your knife, and we'll give you a book of swear-words you've never heard before.'

The same reasoning informs one's dislike of being called by one's first name at the remotest first acquaintance – by some flibbertigibbet salesperson on the phone, for example. The only other treads on the stair beyond this height of intimacy are your nickname and a term of endearment used perhaps by only one person. So if by any remote chance you ever wish to develop the relationship with the FS, where do you go?

The conventions of politeness allow the UL to survive. If we were brutally honest (and perhaps if we know the teller well enough, we are) we would say: 'Come off it, I heard that last week/years ago, and it didn't happen in Troon/Llantwit Major, it happened in Market Harborough/Bootle to a friend of *mine*. Sometimes, the anaesthetic of the teller's claiming the story to be true robs us of all memory of having heard it before. When I began to note down ULs, I soon noticed myself taking a different attitude to anecdotal conversation, and those who have discussed the work have remarked the same thing.

So unless one has the right relationship with someone, it is not possible to laugh in his face and call his veracity into question. And the affectation of kinship with the protagonist of the story both lends verisimilitude to an otherwise bald and unconvincing narrative, and protects the teller.

In 'Jokester', a short story by Isaac Asimov, the author suggests that sense of humour was bestowed on the race by extraterrestrial watchers. The gift, it was alleged, was a control in a giant experiment – jokes were introduced by the experimenters, and as long as the subjects kept laughing, it was known that they hadn't rumbled that they were being observed. One day, it was realised that jokes were never seen in creation, laughter stopped, so did the experiment. Convoluted.

The late Dudley Clews (mathematician and cornettist) decided to invent a joke, tell it to someone at Land's End, and catch it when it arrived at John O'Groats. But inventing a new joke, with the uniqueness necessary for this experiment, is far from easy. It came to him very early in the morning, and, with that adrenal excitement which accompanies such invention, he had to rush out and tell someone. He banged on a neighbour's door and the victim, unaware of the privilege that was being bestowed on him, listened blearily and unwillingly to Dudley's story. At the end, Dudley waited expectantly for the deserved acclaim. All he got was: 'Piss off, you daft bugger, you made it up!' (SLAM) The really interesting thing would be to know what the story was, but to our lasting regret, we never found out. But the tale lives on, to be recounted with fond memories whenever two or three of us gather.

One of the features of stories told and retold is that they become embroidered and intermingled. The Cambridge psychologist Dr Alice Heim's first-ever paper (1936) was 'An Experiment in Humour'. She told 32 stories – some of which were funny – to 50 subjects, and recorded their reaction to the humour. (I asked her if she could remember any of the stories, which are not enshrined in her paper, but unfortunately she couldn't.) However, the really interesting thing about the experiment was that, when she interviewed the subjects again after six months, and asked them if they could remember any of the jokes, she found, *inter alia*, that she got some new – and sometimes even better – jokes, compounded of parts of other jokes, which had not always been in the original list. I have noticed that this is one of the strange tricks that the human mind plays, and one of the ways in which the UL develops.

Embroidery of stories can take place on several levels. At its simplest, it is the 'friend' to whom it happened, when in fact it was a foaf. By claiming the friendship, the teller draws his tale one step nearer to reality. The next stage of broderie is to name the friend, or at least to identify the friend as 'a chap I used to work with'. On the same plane, I think, is to name the place at which the incident happened – and this will have to suit the teller, such as: 'When I was in Truro a couple of years ago . . . '

As we progress up the stages of broderie, the tale itself becomes modified, new heights of nast being added according, as I've said, to the teller and his audience. And the thought can become the deed.

Suppose you think: 'One day, I'm going to put a grinning, maniacal mask on the back of my head, go for a drive, lean out of the window when I overtake someone, and give him a fright.' The idea is neither brilliant nor novel; Harpo Marx performs a variant of it in *Monkey*

Business (1931) and I first heard of a foaf doing it in the early fifties. However, that is the basis of the idea, but the imaginative teller sees some difficulty in frightening an overtakee because of the geometry of the manoeuvre, so he uses a left-hand drive car. Having got thus far, the frightened overtakee can do one of several things – he can take the foaf's number and report him to the police, he can run into a ditch, or he can have a heart attack. The prankster may use a gorilla mask – something to do with *Morgan – a Suitable case for Treatment* (1966)? – and the whole incident may occur abroad, since it is well known that abroad all roads have a sheer precipice on one side. In that case, as like as not, the victim's car bursts into flames, and he is fried.

Now, all these details I have added to the basic story may have been derived, consciously or subconsciously, from other stories, plays, films – indeed from anywhere, in my experience. When I first heard the 'finger in the door' story (p 178), it didn't have the added refinement of the attacker being traced by the police. I took that refinement, and added it to the mask story above. When I first heard the 'headless motor-cyclist' story (p 177), it had no heart attack in it. That was another addition which I borrowed, and grafted on to the mask story. And so on.

Enough of this. Why read menus and cookery books when you can eat the food? Read on, and *bon appetit*.

I

Mistaken Identity

The man who never made a mistake never made anything.
— *Old Excuse*

A mishearing can be completely innocuous, but it can easily lead to sulks, punches-up or even death. An innocuous example:

Speaker: What a *bonne idée*.
Hearer: What a bonny day.

Or a lady in a shop:

'Do you have any of that local Esterol cheese?'

Or something I heard recently, to my initial puzzlement:

' . . . the head-on-a-stick atmosphere of the twenties.'

Another, recounted by George Melly, concerned an argument he was having with Ian Christie wherein the latter averred that George's thought patterns were the result of his middle-class background.' George agreed 'that this might be true, but that it was after all an accident where any of us were *dropped from the womb*.'

'Don't try and confuse the issue with that Surrealist bollocks,' shouted Ian. George was puzzled and asked Ian what he found Surrealist in what he'd been saying. It turned out that Jan thought that George had said 'lopped off the moon'.

A later George mishearing concerns the manager of the hotel in which he was staying asking:

'Is your suite comfortable?'
'What does *he* want?' asked George.
'Who?'
'The Chief Constable.'

Ripley reports 'A Tragic Mistake':

In 1831, during Napoleon III's *coup d'etat*, when an aide reported that the mob was facing the Imperial Guard, Count de St Arnaud, who was just troubled with a cough, exclaimed: '*Ma sacrée toux!*' (My damned cough!) This the aide understood to mean *massacrez tous!*' (massacre everybody!) The order to fire was given and thousands of human lives were lost.

If people hear, or see, something which is not there – and this is often wishful thinking* – we may see the birth of a UL. Similarly, they may not hear or see something which *is* there.

A foaf went up and down a street in London, asking for pawpaw – the fruit of *Asimina triloba*. At last she received the reply: 'Sorry, we don't have pawpaw, but we can let you have some Kit-e-Kat.'

The mother of a foaf is an inveterate traveller. One day, she wandered up a mountain track somewhere in Europe, and found herself at a frontier post. Naturally, she was asked to produce her 'papers'; she searched in her handbag, but found that she had left her passport behind in her hotel. On an impulse, she pulled out her Post Office Savings Book (those were the days) and offered it to the guard. He studied it carefully, turning over the pages. Then he looked at her. 'You. You are always visiting Ondemand. This will make a pleasant change.' He stamped the book, and handed it back to her with a smart salute.

To save time, it was customary for the driver of a coach crossing the border to collect the passengers' passports and hand them to the guard. And this occasion was no different – until the unsmiling guard, armed to the teeth, came on board the coach with the passports and called out sternly 'Mrs XYZ'. In fear and trembling, Mrs XYZ stood up. 'Good afternoon madam. My colleagues and I would like to wish you a very happy birthday.' And suddenly everyone burst out singing.

The wife of a foaf returned from a shopping expedition to find a bottom sticking up from under the kitchen sink. 'It's about time you cleared that, you lazy sod,' she shouted, patting the protruding posterior playfully. 'I'm very sorry, madam,' mumbled the plumber, emerging. 'Your husband telephoned me last week, but I wasn't able to come until today.'

Other versions of this hilarious happening are found. It is a caravan

---

* After someone close has died, have you not seen them but fleetingly in the street?

site. The wife returns from shopping to find her husband, wearing a shirt and nothing else, bending over the basin. Playfully she grabs a handful from behind: 'Ding, ding,' she laughs. Well, one caravan looks very like another . . .

College rooms are – or certainly were – notoriously cold. Many years ago, it is said, my zoology supervisor at Queens' College, Dr Ramsay, hit on a way of conducting comfortable supervisions – comfortable for him, that is. He acquired an electrically-heated flying suit in which to cocoon himself, while his pupils shivered. One day, he left the suit to warm up while he went to transact some other business before the start of the supervision. He was delayed; something went wrong with the thermostat and the suit started to smoulder. The first supervisee arrived, knocked, entered, and saw what he took to be the smouldering remains of the don on the chair. Hysterically he raised the alarm – just as the good doctor returned. The student took one look at the 'ghost' and passed out cold.

Certain actors are well-known for their love of the bottle. One such met a friend of his in The Salisbury (St Martin's Lane) and they drank right through the lunchtime. At last, our actor says that he's on in a play at the New Theatre, and why doesn't his friend come along and see it? 'Thanks very much,' replies the friend, and together they roll along to the Theatre, and up to the Dress Circle – where there's plenty of room. The house lights go down and the play starts. After a time our actor turns to his friend and says: 'You're going to enjoy this bit: this is where I come on.'

This same actor (presumably) was on another occasion on tour with a Shakespearean company, and this time managed to appear, on the stage, though again in an unworthy condition – tight as Andronicus as they say in the trade. Off he went:

> 'Now is the wister of our dincontest
> Made glorious Yorkshire by the summer sun
> And all the clous that loused upon our housed
> In the deep . . . the deep . . . bosom . . . '

The audience began to murmur, and a voice shouted: 'You're pissed!'

The Duke of Gloucester (afterwards King Richard III) rolled down to the footlights and swayed glazedly at the house. 'You're quite correct,' he enunciated, 'but just wait until you see the Duke of Buckingham.'

Every age has produced its reputedly drunk actor, and the stories are much the same.

There was a drag artiste who used to nip around to a certain pub between shows for a pint, and one evening it was the landlady's birthday, so she asked him to return for a drink with her after the show. 'I'll come and do you a turn, Ducky,' promises the performer, and returns to the theatre. At the end of the evening he's as good as his word, goes back to the pub and a good time is had by all until the small hours. He emerges into the street, and then the awful truth dawns: the theatre has long since been locked up, and there he is, standing in his transigear as this awful woman, trying to explain in an abnormally deep voice to a taxi-driver that he hasn't any money on him, but if he'll take him back to his flat . . .

People often dream (so it seems) that they are naked in some public place (froid is the word for it) but – luckily – nobody notices them.

Similarly, being taken very short, they at last manage to find a lavatory, discovering only later that it was in a shop window display, and they'd given a public performance. Alternatively, the public place might turn out to be a stage set, an occurrence which has more than once been employed by writers of humorous fiction.

A foaf went into a pub in Ipswich for the first time. The landlord seemed vaguely familiar. 'Don't I know you?' enquired the man. After some discussion, it transpired that the landlord (who was new to Ipswich) had kept a pub in the City near the place where the foaf used to work. It was all the more embarrassing and painful: one day, the foaf had rushed into the Saloon Bar, slammed down his hat and briefcase, ordered a whisky and said he was bursting for a pee. The landlord had told him to 'go through there and turn left', pointing to a doorway. So he'd rushed through there, turned left, pulled out his apparatus as he flung through the door – and found himself giving a display on a platform in the Public Bar. As a result, he was thrown out by the other barman. Shaking with righteousness, he had gone back to the Saloon Bar for his hat and briefcase, and the other barman, who was telling the landlord what had happened, saw him, shouted 'that's the man' and before he could say 'Noilly Prat' he'd found himself in the street again.

A foaf is a barmaid, over six feet tall. Although used to the humorous comments that her stature engendered, she became extremely tired of them. One evening, after a hard day, she snapped on being asked the meteorological question for the umpteenth time – 'What's the weather like up there?' 'It's raining,' she replied, pouring a pint of bitter over the enquirer's head.

A foaf is a consultant gynaecologist in Harley Street. One day, he received the wife of an Indian prince, who desperately wanted children but had been unsuccessful over the years of her marriage: she was visiting the foaf, she said, because she had heard that he was the best in London and, therefore, in the world. He received this news with his customary modesty, asked her many questions, took copious notes. Then he indicated a screened couch in the corner of the consulting-room: 'Would you go over there please, take off your clothes, and lie on the couch?'

'Oh no!' she wailed. 'I want an *Indian* baby.'

It is sometimes politically inopportune for certain public figures to die when they do – and so it was, it was said, for Queen Alexandra. In order to prove that she was still alive (after her death) she was, according to legend, propped up in her carriage and driven through the streets of London with a cord tied to her wrist so that she could be made to wave to the crowds. Why could they have not used a look-alike? Yet many public figures (including Russian Presidents?), it is said, have been set up in this way.

A foaf who is a Readymix® driver suspected his wife of infidelity. One day, he made sure that she thought he was going to be miles away, and then drove past his house. Sure enough, the bedroom curtains were drawn, and outside stood a brand-new Triumph convertible. Sickened at this display of opulence, our driver had a brilliant idea on the spur of the moment – he drove round the block and prepared his load of cement. Then he returned, positioned his lorry, extended the chute, reversed the barrel and filled the Triumph convertible with Readymix. As he packed up to drive away, a foxy little man came out of his house, climbed on to a bicycle, and pedalled briskly away. (As told, the tale sometimes ends ' . . . and pedalled briskly away *in the opposite direction*.' This doesn't seem to make sense, but it underlines the mistake.)

A man reached the magic age of forty and, feeling that life was just beginning, bounded downstairs to breakfast and the bosom of his family. Unfortunately, however, neither his wife, nor his children, seemed to have remembered his milestone so, somewhat crestfallen, he made his way to the office. Here, he was greeted fulsomely by his secretary; this made him feel so much better that he invited her out to a celebratory lunch, which they duly enjoyed. It was then but a small step to her flat for coffee, and her suggesting that she should 'go and change'. So she went and changed – and came back bearing an enormous birthday cake with 40 candles, accompanied by the boss's family . . . and there he was lying completely naked on the sofa.*

Following another birthday treat, a young couple returned to the girl's parents' house to find it in darkness. A message in the hall told them that the house was theirs for a day or two, so they went upstairs and undressed. Just then, the telephone rang; it was the girl's mother asking if she'd let the cats out of the utility room and feed them. 'I'll carry you downstairs,' said the boy – since they were both naked, it was rather exciting. When they reached the hall, all the lights went on to a rousing chorus of 'Happy Birthday to You' from the assembled family and friends.

The girl fainted, and has spoken not a word since: she sits in a chair staring to the front and has to have everything done for her. The boy streaked out of the house – naked – and has never been seen again from that day to this.

A foaf runs the library-book distribution service for a Northern county. One day, he had an urgent telephone call, saying that a consignment of books for distribution to a number of branch libraries had been hijacked. He couldn't understand it at all – who could these thieving bibliophiles be? Then news started to come in from the police – boxes of his books were being found dumped all along the East Lancs Road. Suddenly the whole thing became clear – the books were packed in reject Johnnie Walker boxes from a nearby paper-converting plant.

---

* Since I first heard it, this UL has been encapsulated in a television advertisement – as, indeed, has the one about the seventh-floor dog following its ball, thrown by the boy-friend, out of the window.

A Canadian visitor to New York City was warned about people 'accidentally' bumping into him – they might well be pickpockets. So when somebody *did* bump into him on the sidewalk he immediately felt in his pocket where he usually carried his wallet. It wasn't there. 'Stop, thief!' he shouted, giving chase, 'Give me back my wallet.' He caught up with the bumper who threw him the wallet and made off. Feeling both clever and relieved at having retrieved his stolen goods, he returned to his hotel and ordered himself a drink. It was then that he discovered that he had two wallets.

An elderly lady went shopping with a £5 note (which shows that the story is elderly as well). She took a train to town and during the journey nodded off to sleep. When she woke, she found another elderly lady in the compartment, also asleep. She took out her purse to check her shopping list, and her £5 note was gone. On an impulse she looked into her companion's bag and there on top – no attempt to hide it – was the £5 note. She removed it quietly, for she had no intention of getting the her into trouble, and left the compartment. After her day's shopping, she was met by her husband at the station. 'However did you get all that stuff?' he asked. 'You left your £5 note on the mantelpiece.'

Almost as soon as I arrived in Chicago in 1978, I found myself sitting in on the piano with Jim Beebee and his Chicagoans, enjoying the extraordinary running commentary of the legendary drummer Barrett Deems. Jim told me of a fellow bandleader who had become progressively madder and richer at the same time because a member of the audience had insisted that the band play *Basin Street Blues* all the evening. This punter was paying $500 a time for each performance and, even if the band had grown tired of playing the same tune over and over again, word had gone round that he was a big noise in the underworld and that his Rolls-Royce, parked outside, was full of gunmen.*

---

* Serendipity again; today (101104) I read the obituary of 'society' bandleader Lester Lanin (1907–2004): 'Lanin would play until 5.30am, if required. One American plutocrat, Charles Tandy, pressed wads of money into Lanin's hand to keep the music going. When the last chord was finally played, Tandy collapsed on the dance floor; he died the following day.'

A foaf visits an Arab Prince to negotiate some enormous deal. At the conclusion of the interview, he stands up, saying: 'Your Highness, I appear to have dropped my wallet containing half-a-million dollars.' 'On the contrary,' observes the Prince suavely, 'the wallet you have dropped should contain a million dollars.'

'Facilitation payments' are part of that culture, but I heard of a civil engineering foaf whose negotiations somehow went wrong to the extent that, in retaliation, his firm supplied the plans, but not the elevations, for an elaborate flyover. 'And, do you know, they built it on the level, and then wondered why they kept having massive crashes.'

A true story: in 1984, I went to Saudi Arabia to research a history of Saudi Telecom. One of my interviewees was Ahmed Zaidan, a charming and venerable Arab who had been attached to the Marconi Company at Chelmsford in the twenties to learn all about wireless; he had then returned as personal wireless operator to King Saud, travelling all over the Kingdom. He regaled me with hospitality and fascinating stories. At last I presented my all-but- superfluous letter of introduction – written all in squiggle – explaining that the Minister of Posts and Telephones had asked my employer to prepare a history of Saudi Telecom. Ahmed Zaidan studied the letter and handed it back to me with a wry smile: 'On the contrary, it is your employer who has suggested to the Minister that you should prepare the history.' My perceptions flipped.

A woman goes to a bank for a loan so that she can extend the family house. The bank manager asks if she has any collateral. She says she has a few ancient share certificates in her deceased father's old oak chest: she guesses they are worthless. But one of them turns out to be an original certificate issued in 1892 by Standard Oil of New Jersey (or some such), which is now some gigantic multinational company: that one share has split four hundred times and is now worth hundreds of thousands of dollars.

But a straightforward story of honesty is not very interesting; it needs embroidery:

A foaf buys two tickets in a lottery – one for himself and one for a colleague at the office. However, he forgets to give the ticket to his colleague and, inevitably, one of the tickets wins the first prize. It is the one he had planned to give to his colleague and he is so honest that he hands it over. 'Thanks very much', says the colleague, pockets a cool £5.4M and is never seen again.

The National Lottery has given rise to its ULs – men who divorce their wives so that they can secretly claim the jackpot they have won; people who forget to buy the ticket with the (winning) weekly number choice and then have to face their syndicate; people who suddenly realise they have a substantial win to collect and arrive at the office just after the three months' grace has elapsed.

In the early days of the Lottery, before it was understood that the central database knows which tickets were bought where, and when, there were tales of dogs and babies chewing up 'winning' tickets, and tickets falling in the fire, not to mention tickets bought retrospectively, or sets of numbers put through the washing machine and glued into winning configurations.

There are numerous stories of people receiving social security payments to pay for colour television sets, running cars and – most mind boggling – continental holidays; sometimes the tales are contrived to fit the 'rules' regarding supplementary benefit, or 'rules' are invented to make an indignant story. For instance, it is said to be possible to use a furniture grant to buy a television set, provided that the set stands on its own legs and has a door in front of the screen. A still more preposterous refinement has been added to the myth that cars are available to some lucky claimants.

In Yorkshire a car dealer rang the local social security office to check if it was in order to exchange a car for a supplementary benefit draft 'because the chap here says that once you put a seat cover inside the car, the seat becomes a settee, and therefore a piece of furniture'.

But not even the dole is the great leveller, for marching shoulder to shoulder with these stories of opulence we are told that:

> . . . there is a new breed of thieving geriatrics pinching bread and milk to survive, and the odd tin of grade two rock salmon, to put on a bit of a show when their grandchildren come to tea. They're too proud to admit to their children that they're on the breadline. It's symptomatic of the society we've produced that skiving, malingering drop-outs can manage to cheat the country legally, while previously virtuous, upright people at their wits' end are mistakenly resorting to a bit of thieving on the side to make their lives bearable.

So how is anyone to make a living? Many years ago, before the framing of the rules that now control newspaper advertising, a man placed an advertisement in a paper offering ex-government trousers for some ludicrously low price. The orders rolled in, he banked the money, and did nothing else. Then letters asking what had happened to the orders started to roll in, and still he did nothing. But whenever he received a threat, solicitor's letter, *etc*, he went out and bought a pair of trousers and sent it to the complainant. But most of the people didn't bother to pursue him, and he became very rich. The low price that had attracted them in the first place was hardly worth the bother of recovery.

A lady was travelling to hospital by bus; on arrival she found that her specimen had been stolen. Why? Well, the only vessel she had been able to find was a Haig whisky bottle.

Having got that far, I was delighted to find another foaf who had left the specimen in her bicycle basket: rather than steal it, the remover (said to be a GI – it was during the war) had left a couple of £1 notes and a thank-you card.

Another foaf spent a good deal of money on some hash and whisky, sold to him by an Arab. The 'hash', however, turned out to be dried camel dung, so he was in two minds about the 'whisky'.

He could always have done as a friend of mine did – try it on someone else. This friend was told, in great glee, by an obnoxious colleague of how he had peed into a bottle of drink in order to pay someone back. Now, this obnoxious colleague had a bottle of sherry which he would produce from his usually locked filing cabinet only when an important client visited. One day, my friend found the cabinet open! . . . and peed into the bottle. The next important client (who happened to be an expensive woman) accepted a glass of sherry. 'Hm,' she said 'rather . . . unusual.' She seemed to enjoy it. Obnoxious guessed what had happened – but took it like a man.

I am indebted to the late Mrs Janie Gothard* for the following:

---

* I found her in the *East Anglian Magazine* where through I corresponded with her before finding that she lived just down the road! Similarly, I carried on a lengthy correspondence with a publisher, and eventually went to London to meet him, only to find that he lived in the next village but one.

The parcel of dried fruit for the anniversary cake duly arrived from Australian cousins, with no note or letter. The ingredients, including some greyish powder – to add spice? – were duly mixed and baked, and the cake pronounced by family and friends as 'gorgeous'.

Then the delayed letter arrived, with the instructions: 'By the way, the grey powder in the packet is Uncle Joe's ashes. Would you please scatter them on his mother's grave?'

In the first (and slightly more credible) version I heard of that, the ashes arrived in a cocoa (or some such) tin, and were put to use because the foafs thought that it was some new Australian brand.

Knowing that the masses will eat – and, worse, *prefer* – such food, is it any wonder that experienced chefs become a little annoyed when their masterpieces do not receive the appreciation they deserve?

Clive Sinclair told me that he had once had a holiday job as a waiter, and recalled an instance when a customer sent back a dish of food, complaining that it was cold. 'Cold?' shouted the irate chef. 'COLD? I'll give him cold,' and he spat into the food, stirred it round and commanded my friend to take the food back. The customer thanked him, said that it was 'much better now' and, of course, ate it.

I understand that chefs do chew garlic and spit it into the food. Presumably they can't fiddle about with effete aids such as garlic crushers. While in Germany I did see with my own eyes (and who else's?) the German chef in the mess kitchen spit into a pot. I didn't know whether it was macerated garlic or Anglophobia.

Another friend told me of the wise old Cheesemaster who retired from the dairy at some advanced age, whereafter the local speciality cheese (Esterol?) never tasted the same. So they called him back and checked all their procedures against his fund of knowledge. At length the secret was revealed; it had been his practice to chew some particularly virulent tobacco and spit it in at the appropriate stage in the process.

Probably most art has now been replaced by science (although 'science' usually means 'technology' in this context). Tales such as that of the wise old Cheesemaster are particularly rife whenever some industry is in transition, presumably once again to 'prove that those scientists don't know everything'.

So the wise old Steelmaker, who knew just when to pour the steel by the changing colour of the flame roaring from the Bessemer converter, and who was retired when the plant was automated, had to be brought back by the crestfallen manager who just couldn't get things to work properly. And more often than not, there was some 'secret ingredient' that had been left out of the process. The secret ingredient was often 'bull's urine', another example of sympathetic magic!

The wife of a foaf was having trouble cleaning the lavatory, so she put some strong acid down it and went out shopping. The foaf returned home unexpectedly in order to use the loo somewhat violently: the acid splashed his bottom, and his wife returned to find him writhing on the floor. She immediately sized up the situation, doused her spouse liberally with water and telephoned for an ambulance. When the ambulance men were told what had happened, they laughed so much that they dropped the stretcher and broke the foaf's leg.

It is a fact of life which, no doubt, many Mrs Grundies see as a momentary lapse in the creator's scheme of things, that what goes in must come out, generally in some unpleasant form. After all, if the body doesn't want it, neither does anyone else.

It is therefore in line with the nature of the process that various unpleasant things should happen to friends, their occurrence giving the raconteur an excuse for speaking of the unspeakable.

A professor (so it *must* be true) who used a public lavatory in Nottingham found that he could not remove himself from the seat. After making suitable efforts and wondering what he should do, he called the attendant who, once he had gained entry, ascertained that the professor was stuck to the seat with superglue – the work of vandals. A mechanic was called in to unscrew the seat, and an ambulance to take the prof and the seat to hospital. When the ambulance men arrived they laughed so much that they dropped the stretcher, causing the professor to further suffer a broken leg.

These vandals, perhaps, were those who later stretched cling-film across the top of the pan, with mind-boggling effect.

A foaf was not feeling well, but just couldn't see how he could miss the office Christmas party, so he took the train to town and over-indulged himself enormously, with the result that he was really very ill in several directions at once. So he stumbled into an army surplus shop on his way back to the station, asked for a pair of trousers – '38 waist, quick, here's a Faraday' – the assistant stuffed them into a bag, and the foaf just managed to scramble into an empty compartment on the corridorless train back home. He removed his mucky old trousers, rolled them up, and threw them out of the window. Then he opened the bag, and found that somehow he had bought a denim jacket.

A foaf is a vet in Saudi Arabia. A friend of his out there was in charge of building a school: top-class stuff, no skimping. After a time, however, the cesspit filled up, and on inspection the cause was found to be lots and lots of little stones. The architect conferred with the headmaster and found that the local custom was to use stones rather than lavatory paper. The pit was cleared, and the headmaster discussed the matter with the school, explaining that with this system, one had to use paper. However, the cesspit filled up again. This time, each stone was found to be wrapped in a piece of paper . . .

When we first moved to Histon (1954), we had a cesspit which seemed to need constant emptying – every week Tovey's Sludge Gulper was in attendance at our behest. Then it dawned on us – we were trying to lower the water table.

Later, we lived in the new Cambridgeshire village of Bar Hill, where there were two main phases of building, to be joined as the village was completed. The phases were known as 'up the hill' and 'down the hill', and it was well known to residents of each phase that those in the other (apparently) indulged in continuous wife-swapping parties. This is a very interesting tale, because it appears that similar stories circulate wherever there are two communities in appropriate locations.

At a rape trial, the woman in the case stood in the witness box, and was asked what the defendant had said to her. She gulped a few times, and then whispered: 'I dare not say.' 'Write it on a piece of paper, then,' said the kindly judge. This was duly done, and the paper was passed around the court. It arrived at the jury, and passed silently along the front row, and then the back. However, it was a hot day, and one of the lady jurors had dozed off, so she was somewhat startled to feel a nudge from her male neighbour, and to be passed a piece of paper reading: 'I'm going to screw you like you've never been screwed before.' 'How dare you,' she shouted, and slapped his face.

A version of this is reported where it is the male who is asleep, and, on being handed the piece of paper, hastily stuffs it into his pocket. The judge asks the usher to retrieve the 'evidence', whereupon the man says: 'Oh, no, your honour, that note is a personal matter between the lady and me.' This version is dismissed because of the unlikelihood of a male juror being asleep during the high-spot of the trial – the evidence of the girl. The former version therefore seems the more likely.

A story of passing examinations: a student has to write two essays, but can only tackle one of them, so heshe writes what looks like the ending of the first essay (the one heshe can't do) at the top of a new page, rules it off, and then does the second. The instructor doesn't like to admit that heshe's lost half the answer paper, and marks himmer by doubling hisser score for the 'second' essay – which gives himmer a top grade.*

A variation of this is to hand in the answers you can do, take the other part of the paper away and complete it as quickly as possible, then slip it on the floor at the back of the class and wait for it to be found and handed in.

In a third variety, the examiner receives a letter obviously intended for the examinee's mother, and mother appears to get the answers, which she then appears to mail to the examiner. Clearly this won't work unless you are being examined by post.

(Hint: if you want to cut off a boring telephone conversation, stab the switch while *you* are in full flow. It never fails.)

---

* Political correctness. Arncher heartily sick of it? Hasn't it made that story about the two essays a pain? Suppose I made it 'he' throughout – would someone complain that it was male oriented? But would members of the fairer sex (!) really complain if they were omitted from all those stories wherein the protagonist appears in a poor light? I'll stick to the good, old-fashioned, inclusive male pronoun, and don't you worry your pretty little heads about it. There's a similar problem encountered by those preparing brochures. In the old days, the male sat at a desk, with the female secretary standing. Then the female sat at the desk, but the standing male still looked dominant. The problem was not made easier when one of the parties had to have a dark skin.

A housewife in Selly Oak went to fetch in her milk one morning, and there on the step was a shabby carry-cot containing a little dark baby with a note pinned to the moth-eaten blanket: 'Please look after me.' Now, this lady badly wanted to adopt a child, so she took the carry-cot into the house. Just then her husband came down, took one look at it and put his foot down: 'Oh no, we're not having *that*,' and he called the police. A car arrived, and a policeman and policewoman got out and came to investigate the foundling. What had at first sight appeared to be a mattress turned out to be a pillowcase. And it was stuffed with wads of £50 notes.

A critic went to see a play, and turned in his piece the next day. The editor was far from pleased when he found that his rivals had reported the play in a rather different way, for it appeared that one of the actors had been accidentally stabbed during a duel. He called in his critic. 'How did you come to miss this story?' he thundered. The critic drew himself up to his full height. 'Sir,' he replied, 'I am the drama critic, not a crime reporter.'

That's just one manifestation of the incompetent reporter. In other versions, he goes to see the beginning of the play, then gets detained at the bar and misses the stabbing. In another version, he just gets detained at the bar, and misses the reality of the curtain getting stuck, or the theatre burning down, or whatever it is that happens. Sometimes it's not the dramatic critic. It may be the music critic, or the sports reporter who writes the report of the concert, or game, before it takes place, only to find after turning in his piece that the game has been cancelled, or rained off. Since most games (like most pieces of music) have a score of some sort, I find it difficult to understand how this one works.

Photogravure magazines, colour supplements and the like are printed well in advance. There is a story of a well-known magazine which prepared an account of a Hollywood wedding but on the very day it hit the streets, the divorce was announced.

There was a poor Neapolitan family, working in the north of Italy. The father died, and the family wished to return him to his native soil; however, they found that the cost of taking a coffin from north to south was far beyond their slender means. So they dressed him in his Sunday suit, and took him south by train, sitting between his two eldest sons.

For some reason, both had to get out at a station, and nearly missed the train. However, they just managed to clamber on to the last carriage and fell into the gangway. They made their way along to the front carriage, and found that the old man had disappeared. There was the most terrible scene, knives flashed, and eventually the frightened family in the compartment confessed. Apparently the train had started with a jolt, and a heavy suitcase had fallen down on the old man who had, of course, fallen forwards on to the floor. They examined him – 'Mama mia! He's dead! And it was *our* suitcase that had killed him.' So they had thrown the body off the train.

A lady and her daughter were travelling on the Continent, and arrived at an hotel in Paris as their last stop on the way home to England. They retired to their separate bedrooms and the daughter, who was especially tired after supervising all the luggage, dropped off to sleep almost immediately, and did not wake until late in the morning. She rose, and went to the door which connected her room to her mother's, but found it locked – so she went round by the corridor and knocked. There was no reply. She spoke to the hall porter, the assistant manager, the manager, and all told the same story; that she had arrived alone, not with her mother; the insinuation was that she must be losing her reason. They showed her the room where she alleged that her mother stayed the night, and the furniture and décor were quite different.

Being made of stern stuff, she calls the police and, gradually, the truth is unearthed – after she had gone to bed, her mother had been taken ill and called the doctor. The doctor had recognised that mother was suffering from cholera, and would surely die. Not wishing to lose all his guests and his reputation, the manager had insisted that the woman was removed from his hotel, the room was quickly redecorated and refurnished, and the whole staff sworn to secrecy.

Folklorist Katherine Briggs quotes this story; she refers us to Woollcott (although she erroneously calls him 'Northcott')'s *While Rome Burns* (1934), and also to the film *So Long at the Fair* (1950; set at the time of the 1889 Paris Exposition). Woollcott found that it was in a novel by Mrs Belloc-Lowndes *The End of the Honeymoon* (1913) and in another by Lawrence Rising *She who was Helen Cass*, and traced it back in various guises to the *Detroit Free Press*, 1889. Woollcott puts his finger on the essence of the UL in referring to this one:

For such a story to travel round the world by word of mouth, it is necessary that each teller of it must believe it true, and it is common practice for the artless teller to seek to impart that belief to his listeners by affecting kinship, or at least a lifelong intimacy, with the protagonist of the adventure related.

It's believable in an hotel, since they're used to changing things round at the drop of an hat – beds come and go, dining rooms change to exhibition halls, here today and gone tomorrow. Elsewhere, modular shopfitting has its part to play. The Pharmacy in Ely Tesco had to close; there it was one day, and no trace whatsoever the next.

Just as people sometimes disappear without trace, so do they sometimes appear without parentage. There is, for example, the famous economist Milton Keynes, one of the rising young men of the 1920s. Albert and Lady Margaret Hall are a famed couple. And it was a pity to have missed the concert given by Viola da Gamba and her harpsichord. Denys Parsons quotes the *Nottingham Daily Express*:

> We have printed, verbatim, all that Phillimore gives on the subject. Nor has Phillimore rested his facts on Prideaux alone. He quotes Ibid as his authority for paragraphs 3 and 4, both of which paragraphs confirm paragraph 2 based on Prideaux.

I have always wanted to start a publication called *Ibid*. However, when in the RAEC in Germany (attached to No 1 Wireless Regiment, 1954–5), I was faced each month with having to set the Third Class Army Certificate of Education English paper. One of the obligatory questions was always a comprehension test, based on a newspaper report.

One month, we were completely unable to find a suitable paragraph so we concocted one from a fictitious publication called *Orb and Sceptre*. How gratifying to think that a copy of this examination paper is somewhere enshrined in the BAOR archives. *Caveat lector*.

Just as bombs were reported as having been dropped at Random, so it was reported that the Germans had surrendered En Masse. More than twice have I heard on the news of Welsh accident victims being taken to the Ysbyty Hospital, where they are in a stable condition.

And somewhere along the line, a visiting lecturer who had attended

Queen's College, Oxford, and been granted an honorary MA degree was described reverently as 'Master of the Queen's Oxen.'

Also in Oxford, a student at Christ Church (known as 'The House') said, according to his interviewer, that he 'could see his house from his lodgings'.

No book on ULs would be complete without the vanishing granny, otherwise known as the stolen corpse, oft reported, in numerous guises to suit the occasion yet still (it would seem) believed to be true by both tellers and listeners.

A couple went touring in Spain, and took the wife's mother with them. While on holiday, the old lady died, and they didn't know what to do. They decided to return home at once with the body wrapped in their tent on the roof-rack. Somehow they made it through the customs, drove home as fast as possible, and went indoors for a cup of tea. When they went outside again to fetch the tent, they found that the car had been stolen. And after overcoming the problem of explaining to the police what had happened, they still had another hurdle to overcome – neither car nor granny has been found, and they will have to wait seven years before she can be presumed dead and probate can be granted.

2

Shut Up

> I had walled the monster up within the tomb!
> Edgar Allan Poe, *The Black Cat*

Poe knew full well that walling up things and people is guaranteed to produce a shiver – somehow we need to suspect that under the calm exterior is something hidden and macabre.

Anyone who read at a tender age, as I did, such Poe classics as *The Black Cat*, *The Cask of Amontillado*, or *The Tell-tale Heart*, is hardly likely to forget the tales, even if as the years pass they merge into a certain sameness of plot.

For the walling up of the soul, I would refer you to a lesser-known Poe tale *The Facts in the Case of M Valdemar*. If I may prune the story drastically, M Valdemar was on his deathbed, and the storyteller suddenly realised that no one had 'as yet been mesmerised *in articulo mortis*.' So M Valdemar became the subject of this new experiment. He remained mesmerised for about seven months, until at length 'the same hideous voice, which I have already described, broke forth: "For God's sake! – Quick! quick! – put me to sleep – or, quick! – waken me! – quick! – *I say to you that I am dead*!".'

Our mesmerist of course obliges:

> As I rapidly made the mesmeric passes, amid ejaculations of 'dead! dead!' absolutely bursting from the tongue and not from the lips of the sufferer, his whole frame at once – within the space of a single minute, or even less, shrunk – crumbled – absolutely *rotted* away beneath my hands. Upon the bed, before the whole company, there lay a liquid mass of loathsome – of detestable – putrescence.

That's the end. It's done one good thing for us – provided the verb 'to Valdemar' which is what happens to certain instant puddings if they're left too long.

People (rightly) find a fascination in the fact that great buildings (cathedrals for example) are honeycombed with passages and rooms of which one would not dream until some concealed door is opened, revealing a glimpse of the works. Museums and art galleries display but a fraction of their possessions: behind doors through which members of the staff disappear with the aid of their jangling pass-keys are massive hoards of treasures, and innumerable offices and workshops.*

Any house with servants' quarters is the same – there is an abrupt change in style and décor which tells you which side of the blankets you're on. Visit the loo as a tourist in many a grand house, and enter a whole new world.

Stories of secret passages and tunnels – or at least rumours thereof – abound wherever there is an old building. There's a passage from the Manor House to the Church. From the Monastery to the Nunnery. Travelling further afield, we find that the Sphinx is a massive secret doorway to an underground system of passages leading to the several pyramids. And it should come as no surprise to find that some believe our very planet to be hollow, or at least a complex labyrinth of passages.

With so much effort having been put into the construction of now-forgotten hiding places, it is natural that they should be unearthed from time to time, with attendant legends.

That doyen of Secret Hiding Places. Granville Squires, wrote:

> Every discovered tunnel is labelled 'secret', when it was never anything of the kind, and nearly every one is said to run to the church. Nobody has ever been able to give an explanation of why it should.

When walled-up things are rediscovered, they would seem to have a habit of crumbling. Usually they stay whole long enough for the discoverers to have a good look at them, and then collapse in a pile of dust. This happened to a roundhead's hat which Charlie Ison said he found while unearthing a priest's hide under the floor of the airing cupboard in my parents' house in Histon. For a moment it was visible in its pristine glory, as fresh as the day it had been put there. Then it crumbled into dust.

---

* Exploring the Royal Academy as its new President, Sir Hugh Casson was delighted to find a door marked 'No Entry' on both sides.

And it adds to the storyteller's armoury of the marks of mystery; according to Ernsting:

> Inside the chamber, close to the threshold, lay four human skeletons, a few colourful rags still attached to the bones. They were ancient. As soon as the draught hit them, they simply fell apart. They must have been lying here for many thousands of years.

In Fellini's *Roma*, an underground railway is being tunnelled (in Rome) and they discover a very beautiful Roman villa. It exhibits some exquisite murals which, even as they gaze upon them, dissolve and run down the walls.

Slow but inexorable, this is the fate of the cave-paintings at Lascaux and elsewhere; we may brood on this as the very epitome of self-destructive art.

Walled up in that great pile which is the University of Manchester Institute of Science and Technology, there is said to be a lavatory built specially for Queen Victoria in case she wanted to open her bowels as well as the building. Whether or not she used it is unrecorded. And whether it was walled up because it was too inconvenient a convenience, or because it was considered too reginal for ordinary use, I don't know either.

Another story of Queen Victoria's movements avers that she was not in favour of lavatories on trains. It was therefore necessary to ensure that there was a supply of suitably-spaced halts along the route of any royal progress. That is why Milton Keynes is where it is; before the railway age there was hardly anything there; then Queen Victoria wished to visit the West country, and a station had to be built at Woburn Sands; hence Milton Keynes. That's what I've heard, anyway.

Another story oft told, especially where there are Sappers in the Mess, is that when royalty visits they place a convenient filter down the royal loo and pot any interesting captures in resin to add to their top-secret collection. They need just one more visit to complete the royal flush. After a great deal of negotiation, they manage to arrange that visit – but unfortunately the visitor doesn't use the loo. No wonder they're pressing so hard for a follow-up visit.

Mysteries, mysteries. According to a reviewer, a book on the Marquis de Sade stated that the British Library holds unpublished de Sade manuscripts 'only to be read in the presence of the Archbishop of Canterbury and two other trustees.' (In fact, that's the publisher's blurb.) In response to the reviewer's inquiry, the keepers at the British Library have given their official assurance that no such manuscripts exist. But we all 'know' that there are such holdings in large libraries – indeed, the tower of the Cambridge University Library is, according to a tradition which cannot be very old (for the building is about my age), 'full of pornography.'

And what about Joanna Southcott's Box? The Panacea Society is always advertising for the Bishops to get together and open the Box. I don't understand why the Bishops don't call the bluff of the Panacea Society – it would make a light-hearted entertainment at an ecclesiastical conference. If the box were found to contain our salvation, the divines would presumably be able to congratulate themselves on their wisdom. If it contained some fatuity, they could all have a good laugh. In either case, the Panacea Society would be saved the expense of all that advertising.

In 1945, Dr Ingram of the Low Temperature Research Institute came to talk to our Science Club at school about the possibility of preserving food by freezing – we were cautious, then delighted, as we sampled strawberries which had been picked before the war. Today, we see no wonder in such things; we merely grumble if the shop has run out of some frozen delicacy, and insure our home freezers against power cuts. For our ULs, we have to turn to more exotic sources, the most well-known of which is of course Siberia, where Russian scientists find mammoths preserved in blocks of ice, hack them out, and eat them. And everyone knows as well that tins of food from Scott's Antarctic expedition were as fit to eat when they were recovered as they had been when they were buried (which may not be saying much).

Such things are not inexplicable, nor yet unbelievable, based as they are on well-tried principles. But what about the pyramids? (What about them?) As anyone with a quarter of an eye for the appropriate sections of bookshops will know, there is tremendous power of some sort which is concentrated by pyramids, and makes people feel more at peace, better able to meditate, get a better night's sleep, *etc*. I tried hanging a cardboard pyramid over the bed, but for some inexplicable reason the string broke and it woke us.

It is not clear which is the cause and which the effect – if indeed there be an effect, or even a cause. Can it be that the pyramids of Egypt are nothing more than power concentrators of some sort? Or was the shape hit upon by common sense, clean-cut and easy to build (it's its own ramp), and lasting for a very long time indeed? Is the power a by-product of the pyramid? We're working on it. Suffice it to say that the power may have given rise to two ULs, or vice versa.

First are the grains of wheat interred in the pyramids of Egypt thousands of years ago, said to have germinated instantly when given the right conditions.

Second is the model said to have been found inside the Great Pyramid – a model representing a landscape with rivers of quicksilver (lovely alchemical name) running through it. And the rivers had been running for centuries. Pyramid power? Perpetual motion? M C Escher? Where is the model now?

The idea of drowned cities – whether in volcanic ash (Pompeii) or water (all too horrendously frequent) – is one to take the fancy, and what more expected than to find stories of their continuing to function in some ghostly way? Walters tells us:

Take a day's journey by boat from Cromer to Harwich, and what is the most striking scene that the coast presents to the astonished gaze? Here and there a steeple-top projects out of the waters: it is all that is left of a once-flourishing little town now buried beneath the swirling tides which are rapidly beating down the cliffs, and year by year getting a little further inland.

Cromer, overlooking the sea, and protected by a double break-water which in time of storm is insufficient to keep the raving waves in check, was once four miles from the coast, and the old town of Shipden lies beneath the sea.

The legend runs that as you stand on the crumbling cliffs you can hear the sweet faint sound of bells rising from the sea depths, and that if you look intently at low tide you can see the shadowy outlines of the whelmed houses which made the Cromer of Centuries ago.

I understood that it was the bells of Dunwich that could be heard, but our source does not mention them, though it is at pains to list the dates of disappearance of the several churches. Certainly, if by some miracle the belfry managed to remain intact such that the bells could swing under water, we should be able to hear them. But that Neptune would so order the waters as to practise change-ringing (*not* to be called The Method) I doubt.

It is, however, a common story, and not confined to this country: Debussy's *La Cathédrale Engloutie* tells of a similar happening. And the erosion of our East Coast, with buildings sliding slowly into the sea, is no joke.

But enough of the inanimate. If we turn to the animal kingdom, and climb the evolutionary tree, we find ULs of the walled-up along every branch.

Some years ago, tall, bouffant, lacquered hairstyles were all the rage (for women, that is). One girl decided after some months that she'd go and have her hair taken down and as the operation proceeded, the hairdresser found that the arrangement was full of maggots.

This was first told to me by the brother of the hairdresser to whom it was said to have happened. Again, it may have been true, but it happened to a lot of other people at the same time. Some people harboured black widow spiders – 'in the midst of life', *etc.* Others – and all must have had peculiarly insensitive scalps – had nests of mice, though I understand that this was a purposefully exotic effect sported by certain ladies at the pre-revolutionary French court – on the other hand, it may have been a misunderstanding, since twists of cloth used as part of the construction were called 'rats' (and smaller ones 'mice').

Certainly, with Queen Elizabeth (the first) taking a bath once a year 'whether she needed it or not' being the height of luxury, it is clear that there have been long periods of history when it didn't need exotic hairstyles to shelter wriggling fauna.

Now that coal is out of fashion, and too precious to be kept in the bath (another UL, *en passant*), people are generally cleaner, and their hair is not so high, in any sense. So the creepy-crawlies were enlisted to support the 'buy British' campaign current at the time.

A lady foaf went to the doctor with an abdominal rash. 'Aha!' said the wise medic, 'have you bought a new skirt recently?' The patient said she had. 'Then I should go home and examine it very carefully,' said the doctor, who must have felt rather like Conan Doyle on a good day. So the patient returned home, and examined the garment very carefully. She noticed some irregularities in the waistband.

Curious, she started to unpick it, and found that it was 'full of lice'. The skirt, of course, had been made somewhere in the Far East.*

When yuccas started to appear in the shops, they were soon accompanied by the tale of the foaf who had bought one and either died, or was saved in the nick of time, from the bite of the deadly spider that had been concealed in it.

A peculiar state of affairs obtains with the spider in the story of Robert the Bruce. I remember quite clearly being told this story at the age of nine – RtB was hiding from his enemies in a cave and, while in there, had plenty of time to reflect on his plight. He also had plenty of time to observe a spider which appeared to be having difficulty in spinning a web. However, with great tenacity the cack-footed arachnid carried on and finally succeeded in constructing its web. RtB was thus inspired, and emerged to lead his people to victory.

Many years later, thirty perhaps, I told my wife this story. Don't ask me how we got round to it, but she was surprised because her version was that RtB had been hiding in the cave, and a spider had

*This story was told to me by my mother, who swore that she knew the person to whom it happened, but she refused to divulge her name, 'in case you go questioning her'.

woven a web across the entrance. Seeing the web, the pursuers assumed that nobody could be in the cave and therefore went away; after a decent interval RtB emerged to lead his people to victory. We could see no reason why both versions were not tenable, and of course they are. Most people to whom I have put the choice agree with my wife's version. Presumably there are my fellows of the class of '42, and others who came under the same tutelage, who go along with my version. Neither DNB nor Eyre-Todd gives either version. I have subsequently found that other folk-heroes have been saved by similar means.

Let us now move from the arthropods to the vertebrates – reptilia for a start. Many of these, notably snakes, crocodiles and toads, exhibit reputed turn-off characteristics which tend to prevent people from getting to know them better.

Snakes have been known to jump from the ground and penetrate passing maidens – see Chapter 3. It's never happened to any foaf of mine, however: when the film *Shivers* (1976; X) was released, I thought it might be only a matter of time, but now I don't think I've ever met anyone who has seen *Shivers*.

Alligators are a more well-known subject of ULs. It seems that it was fashionable to keep pet alligators in New York, so many ladies did. And when their loved pets became too unruly – why, they just flushed them down the lavatory. So it is that the sewers of New York are teeming with enormous alligators, much to the consternation of the sewermen. It could be that, with the dependence of a great city on sewerage system, the alligators are the reason for its periodical grinding to a halt.

But the story is a variant of one of some antiquity, told by Henry Mayhew:

There is a strange tale in existence among the shoreworkers, of a race of wild hogs inhabiting the sewers in the neighbourhood of Hampstead. The story runs, that a sow in young, by some accident got down the sewer through an opening, and, wandering away from the spot, littered and reared her offspring in the drain; feeding on the offal and garbage washed into it continually. Here, it is alleged, the breed multiplied exceedingly, and have become almost as ferocious as they are numerous.

This story, apocryphal as it may seem, has nevertheless its

believers, and it is ingeniously argued, that the reason why none of the subterranean animals have been able to make their way to the light of a day, is that they could only do so by reaching the mouth of the sewer at the riverside, while, in order to arrive at that point, they must necessarily encounter the Fleet ditch, which runs towards the river with great rapidity, and as it is the obstinate nature of a pig to swim against the stream, the wild hogs of the sewers invariably work their way back to their original quarters, and are thus never to be seen.

What seems strange in the matter is, that the inhabitants of Hampstead never have been known to see any of these animals pass beneath the gratings, nor to have been disturbed by their gruntings.

The sewer-hunters, of whom Mayhew was writing, had never seen the wild hogs either.

But sewer rats . . . that's another story. Let us return to reptiles.

> I'd rather soar to death's abode
> On eagle's wings, than 'live a toad'
> Pent in a block of granite.
> James Smith (1775–1839), *Chigwell Revisited*

The number of toads that have crouched patiently in rocks or tree-trunks for goodness knows how long until someone wielding the appropriate tool in the appropriate place strikes open the sarcophagus is legion. According to the UL, the tomb splits, revealing the toad, which then usually 'blinks at the unaccustomed light, and hops slowly away' (*cf* 'crumbling into dust' p 62).

This is an old tale, since experiments to disprove it were carried out at least two centuries ago. But it still lives. Bergen Evans puts it in a nutshell:

> The toad's clammy, corpselike feeling, with its suggestion that it is already dead and hence not subject to mortality, may be the basis for many stories that one hears of a toad's being liberated from the centre of a block of stone or concrete in which he had obviously lived for years, or even centuries, without nourishment or air. In the classic version – one often sees it in the paper, date-lined from some place inaccessible to inquiry – the creature is at

first seemingly lifeless. But he revives in the open air, and, to the astonishment of the excavator, hops away apparently none the worse for his strange experience. Unfortunately for the veracity of the anecdotes, a toad must have air to survive; and even with all the air, food and water that he can desire, he will not survive many years.

Robert L Ripley, whose credulity may have been expediently tuned to his pocket, reported thus:

Old Rip, The Horned Toad

In the lobby of the new court house in Eastland, Texas, may be found the remains of 'Old Rip', a horned toad that lived without food or water for thirty one years. Mr W M Wood of Eastland placed the toad in the cornerstone of the court house in 1897 and took it out alive on 17 February, 1928. Old Rip was alive until January 1930, when he died of pneumonia.

For a possible *modus operandi*, consult Bel and the Dragon.

As for the scientific experiments, it is reported that Dr William Buckland* (1784–1856) built an apparatus comprising 24 stone cells covered with glass panels 12 of the cells were 12" x 5" and were of coarse oolitic limestone; 12 were 6" x 5" and of compact silaceous sandstone. Dr B then took 12 large and 12 small toads, and put them into the cavities, then buried the whole thing in 3 feet of earth. Within 13 months, all the toads in the sandstone and the six small toads in the limestone were dead. The large toads in the limestone died within the next year. So there!

Moving on to mammals, we find that rats (which have the foresight to desert ships destined to sink) are now available which can live in the refrigerated containers used for shipping food. Natural selection has produced a breed of super-rat, with thick fur, which can withstand arctic climes to its obvious advantage.

And thence to cats, especially black ones, of course. In December 1976, two cats were reported to have emerged from a frozen meat container at Peterborough, putting the countryside on red alert

---

* Another of Buckland's claims to fame was eating his way through all the species of the animal kingdom for the sake of science..

because of the danger of rabies. The cats had been laid out, presumed dead, and had disconcertingly risen up and run away. Their colour is unrecorded.

In the days when locomotives had fireboxes, there was a news item from time to time wherein a driver who had taken the *Flying Scotsman* (or some other such long-distance runner) to London had heard an untraceable mewing throughout the journey. When he arrived, he was able to track down the elusive feline and to his astonishment had found that it had travelled all the way *inside the firebox*. I heard a variant, which stated that the animal had travelled the distance *on the connecting rod*. It was always a black kitten. For a plausible story of a long-distance black kitten, consult Driver Earl.

Black kittens suffer the most amazing adventures. They emerge from spin-dryers or washing machines 'somewhat bedraggled, but apparently none the worse for their unusual experience'. They spend weeks in refrigerators while their owners are on holiday. They travel from Land's End to John O'Groats under the bonnet of a motor car, or clinging to the exhaust system (a cat converter?) And, of course, they get walled up. In that strange little film *The Plank* a kitten is nailed under the floor (and let out, let me hasten to add). Brian Rix avers that his cat was unwittingly cemented under the stairs when he moved house, and there were still builders at large.

One wasn't so lucky. A foaf had a cat which, attracted by the sweet smell of the Sunday joint, climbed into the (electric) oven for a feast and was shut in. When the door was opened, there was the crisp, well-cooked body of the cat.

Allow me an ornithological diversion, before I return to the human race. A foaf moved into a new house, accompanied by an army of artisans – carpets were laid, furniture moved in and placed: it all went like a military operation. Not surprising, as the man was a retired staff officer. Precisely at 5.30, knocking-off time, the last pieces of furniture were placed, and the men went away. The family sat in the living-room, stretching their legs, congratulating themselves on their perfect arrangements. It was slightly chilly, so mother went to shut the door, and found that there was a lump under the carpet. However, they hammered it flat, and the door gave no further trouble. Then they discovered that the budgerigar was missing . . .

When this is told, according to the teller and the hearer, the reaction may range from peals of laughter to floods of tears. Aficionados of the

UL, however, just say: 'Have you got the one about the budgie under the carpet?', with the reply: 'Yes, I've heard that in Edinburgh, Frinton and Hythe; sometimes it's a canary, sometimes it's a mouse and doesn't come to light until someone notices a patch of blood.' The budgie under the carpet has even turned up in a radio quiz: 'What would you do if . . . ?

And so to *Homo sapiens*.

I had often heard that the Boulder Dam was full of the bodies of men of whom the Mafia had wished to dispose. It was therefore interesting to find that, when the construction of motorways started, and people could see the pouring of millions of tons of concrete going on around them, the story was soon abroad that luckless workmen were 'always' falling into the shuttering and being lost.

The stories were often embellished by mention of sophisticated X-ray equipment which had allegedly been used (always in vain) to locate the bodies. It was seldom stated whether the workmen

found their way into the concrete by accident or design; although the stories were said to stem from eyewitness accounts, none of the eyewitnesses had, curiously enough, ever attempted to rescue their colleagues.

There can be no doubt that there is little substance in these tales, which perhaps arose when workers for some reason failed to report for duty. Similar tales have cropped up in many other countries – in the USA, for example, it is popularly supposed that the victims of Mafia executions [just as I thought] are disposed of by being entombed in concrete river-piers.

When accidents have occurred on construction sites, strenuous efforts have been made to rescue survivors and recover bodies – as in the case of a bridge collapse at Pasadena, California, on 7 October 1972, when a body was actually recovered from a 100-ton block of cement, and it is very unlikely that any genuine suspicion that a worker had fallen into a mass of concrete would go unheeded.

Yes, I suppose so, if there *were* a suspicion. Even in this super-documented age many people do disappear, and nobody knows where or why. Ask the Sally Army.

Stories of people in walls are of great antiquity. Possibly the earliest, and certainly the grandest, is that ordered by the Chinese Emperor Chin Shi Huang-ti (246–210 BCE), builder of the Great Wall. More than 1,000,000 coolies were buried in the 1500-mile-long structure 'to make it strong . . . And he climaxed a reign of lifelong excesses and cruelty by ordering all his family and kin interred with him alive – after his death'. For the record, that's one coolie every 2.6 yards or so – any such strengthening must have been spiritual rather than mechanical.

How about this one?

In 1569, Geronimo, an Arab living in the city of Algiers, renounced Mohammedanism and publicly professed his conversion to Christianity. The infuriated rulers of Algiers thereupon placed him on the 'Fort of 24 Hours', which was then in the process of construction, and poured cement about him which entombed him within the masonry of the fort.

The slave-monk x, who was Geronimo's teacher, was liberated in 1612, and promptly published a history of Geronimo's martyrdom. When the French conquered Algiers in 1830, Haedo's book was referred to, and under its guidance the actual block within which Geronimo had been immured 250 years previously was located and they removed the remains of the martyr.

Geronimo was canonised by the Catholic Church.

In another place, Ripley says:

Khan Jahan ordered his body interred in a tomb with his right hand protruding from its wall – and for forty years every person who visited the spot shook hands with the dead man.

I wonder what happened then?

Returning dead heroes (and there's nothing like death for making heroes) to their homelands has always been a problem, and has given rise to some particularly nauseating stories.

As a lad, a foaf spent some 18 months helping to re-plumb a country house. The titled lady of the house said to the men, who were living in, that perhaps they might care to earn some money at weekends instead of going to the pub – they could clean the enormous chandeliers in the ball room. She had available a barrel of whisky which could be used for the purpose and which she said she was otherwise going to throw out. Of course, the men agreed; they bought some methylated spirits for the chandelier job, bottled the whisky and drank it themselves.

Afterwards the lady paid them handsomely, and said: 'Of course, the best thing was that we were able to use the whisky for something useful instead of throwing it out. My husband died some years ago in Australia, and that whisky was used to pickle his body when it was brought home for burial.'

According to a very old European legend, an expatriate Italian Jew tried to do a Venetian family a favour by returning the corpse of their son for burial. He took the body to pieces and packed them into a jar with spices and honey. However, when the jar arrived home, it was found that the body was far from complete . . . someone had been tucking into it on the journey.

Hugo Davenport told me this UL:

Some years ago, the father of a friend of mine bought a fairly enormous house in the middle of Bodmin Moor, a sort of Georgian Regency house built on the site of an older farmhouse.

In the capacious cellars they found half a dozen very large barrels. 'Oh, good!' said mother. 'we can cut them in half and plant orange trees in them.' So they set to work to cut the barrels in half but, finding that one of them was not empty, they set it up and borrowed the necessary equipment – funnels and sich from the local pub. The cellar filled with a rich, heady Jamaican odour.

'Rum, by God!' said the father. It was indeed, so they decided to take advantage of some fifty gallons of the stuff before cutting the barrel in half.

About a year later, after gallons of rum punch, flip and butter had been consumed, it was getting hard to get any more rum out of the barrel, even by tipping it up with wedges. So they cut it in half, and in it found the well-preserved body of a man.

People who died in the colonies and had expressed a wish to be buried at home were shipped back in spirits, which was much more effective than brine. Rum, of course, was pretty cheap in Jamaica, but Lord Nelson was sent back in brandy, as befitted a national hero – presumably according to Johnson's dictum: 'claret is the liquor for boys; port for men; but he who aspires to be a hero must drink brandy'.

Henry VI died of dysentery on an inconveniently hot August afternoon. The only way to get him from France to England for burial without considerable embarrassment was to cut him up, seal his insides into a jar, boil the rest in aromatic herbs and ship the whole lot to Westminster Abbey in a lead coffin.

Others' eagerness to enjoy the contents of brandy vats has ended in a more macabre fashion.

A family of four drowned in a 12-foot deep vat of Serbian brandy in Rada-Ljevo, after the head of the family fell in. His son dived to rescue him but was also drowned – along with their wives who tried to pull them out.

If someone falls into a barrel, at least you know where they are – or do you? A friend of mine with a gruesome turn of mind told a story of someone who fell into a bath of boiling acid or some equally unpleasant part of an industrial process, and was never seen again. 'They buried the lot in the end' was the relished conclusion of the tale.

3

Mysteries of Medicine

'Doctor, Doctor . . . people keep ignoring me.'
'I know how you feel – next, please!'
New phobias for old

When I was a boy, medicine was simple. You had spots – it was measles. You had a cough – it was whooping-cough. Lumps were mumps. And so on. There was nothing to suggest that there were more complex conditions.

If you were 'off colour', it was the liver – you were said to be 'liverish'. So my grandfather said, anyway. And his cure? A 'dose of physic'. My father's grandmother's cure was 'a good dose of cascara'. When she died, she left an enormous cupboard of *Casacara sagrada* bottles – empty and full. It was great fun, because the tablets burnt like little fireworks.

Words such as 'cancer' and 'impetigo' were never spoken – it was years before I heard them. And, for me at any rate, the discovery of such conditions coincided with the awakening conscience that the medical profession was not infallible . . . though I may have been put off doctors by our family GP who sought to cheer me up when I was a yowling infant by pretending to bash himself on the head with a mallet.

Much of the practise of medicine is built on a supposed sequence of events riddled with fallacies. P is the patient; D the doctor. First, I should say that the following sequence refers to a 'general feeling of malaise' not to something more definable such as coughing blood or lumps in the breast.

1 P feels unwell
2 P visits D
3 D tells P what's wrong
4 D prescribes a cure
5 P takes the cure
6 P gets better.

The 1—2 link is frequently broken; experience may show that whatever the ailment is, it will have gone before D is able to see P – which in itself should make P think. Making an appointment is therefore tempered not only by the supposed seriousness of the condition, but by factors such as D being on holiday (again!) school half term, the car in dock, an important lunch date and so on.

The 2—3 link is uncertain and changing. In the past, P may have thought that every set of signs and symptoms was related to some diagnosable condition, which in turn had a cure (4—6). This is changing for several reasons. (a) D may be more honest, because (b) P is generally more aware – not only because of numerous media items (both fact and fiction) involving the medical profession, but also because of the easier lay access to medical information (from pamphlets and books, from support groups, and on the web). D has long begun by asking P what P thinks the trouble is, on the grounds that P may know what he wants; now, perhaps, P is better informed. D is also interested in finding out whether P thinks things are worse than they really are. (c) Now that the until-recently-unthinkable American practice of suing for professional negligence has crossed the Atlantic (witness the branches of legal professions setting up in hospital concourses (UGH! – I ask you*), D may be loth to diagnose (in case it is a mis-diagnosis) and may even cop out by sending P to a specialist. Even if the waiting time is such that P gets better spontaneously, P will somehow feel bound to keep the specialist's appointment,† and there are far too many tales of P becoming sucked into the machine and being made *really* ill. Remember this next time you forget you've been eating beetroot when you think you're peeing blood. (d) Now that 'assault' can be anything from brushing anorak sleeves in a crowd upwards, D may be loth to examine P properly. So the consultation goes as follows:

P: Doctor, I don't feel too good.
D: What exactly is the problem?
P: My throat feels a bit sore, and I've got a bit of a headache.

* UGH! Indeed – on the very day that I wrote this, I read that 'accident victims will now have to bring their claims for compensation under "no win, no fee" agreements'. Four years later, it's become too much of a good thing, and lawyers are being warned about ambulance chasing.

† The current fashion for notices in clinics castigating patients who fail to keep appointments may of course reflect the number of spontaneous recoveries during protracted waiting times. They can't have it both ways.

D: Ah yes. (Or, perhaps: ' . . . mmm. I wonder what that could be.')

D can be pretty safe in assuming that whatever it is will go away by itself. However D may, like a fortune-teller, ask some sort of reinforcing question.

D: Have you been working extra hard lately?'

P will feel good on two counts – first, the question implies that D knows what's wrong; second, most people like it to be thought that they work hard.

P: Well, perhaps . . . yes.
D: Hmm. I should ease off a bit if I were you.

Unless P is a known malingerer, D will not want to imply that the visit is wasted. This is the point at which convention demands that a prescription should be written (a) to support the idea that the visit was not a waste of time, (b) to show that D knows what the problem is and (c) has something to cure it.

That 3—4 link clearly has a greater purpose than merely providing a cure. Much has been written about the placebo effect, and bemoaning the fact that bread pills and peppermint water are no longer part of the official placeboid armamentarium. Over-prescription of expensive medication which is not used anyway is one of the great sinks of NHS funds.

The 4—5 link is assumed, but P will not necessarily take the cure, whatever it is; like the abandoned exercise bicycle, it is the mere *possession* of the remedy that confers improvement.

P: Why have you changed my medication?
D: What makes you think I have?
P: The old pills used to wash down the loo with ease; these new ones float.

Which brings us to the final, 5—6, link. It should be clear by now that any improvement in P's condition may well be the result of 'nature taking its course' – as the old wives used to say, and how true that is!

Medicine is seldom a clear-cut sequence of events, of linked causes and effects. Even physical occurrences may not be what they seem; old people fall over and break their femurs – or do they? An old person with osteoporosis may fall over *because* a femur gives way – not the expected sequence at all.

And so that magical rapport, the doctor–patient relationship, has been eroding for some time. Many years ago, an industrial psychologist friend of mine, who made a special study of doctors' interviewing techniques, found himself lecturing jointly on the subject with a top surgeon of the old school. They got together before the meeting for the purpose of comparing notes on what each was going to say. After the introductions, the surgeon blasted my friend: 'You know, the whole trouble is that these days the patients don't call you "Sir" any more' – erosion indeed.

The same friend was on another occasion being shown some work that was being done on using a computer to interview patients. A question appears on the computer screen; the patient types the answer. 'Don't you think,' my friend asked tentatively, 'that the human element is missing from the system?' 'Not at all,' replied the proud progenitor, 'we program the computer to make suitably encouraging remarks from time to time.'

Today, doctors may put their trust in the expert (or knowledge-based) system – equivalent to a vast brain holding the accumulated wisdom of many specialists – a well as the Internet accessible to medics and laymen alike.

The doctor–patient relationship is ticklish; the secret of being a patient is to start in a thoroughly one-down position and gradually find out how far the doctor will let you go. I was once referred to a specialist and, before visiting him, looked him up in the Medical Directory so that I should know what sort of man to expect. The Directory told me of some interesting-looking papers he had written, so I went and looked them up. Although I didn't mean to, I let on far too early in our consultation that I knew something about him. Instead of his being flattered, the information completely upset the D–PR, and nothing came from the referral.

Be that as it may, it is more likely that, as I've hinted, the medical practitioner has been exposed as an ordinary human who has been through some course of training which happened to be medical. As one's experience widens, one begins to understand the extraordinary ambiguity in 'caring' – the patient must be treated as an individual human being, and the carer must understand the continuum between caring and emotional involvement, and how to detach appropriately. Caring without emotional involvement is in itself an emotional strain: no wonder there are high jinks off duty.

Two horrors, kept alive by books about them, are the fear of spontaneous combustion and the fear of being buried alive. Spontaneous combustion is 'a curious belief that had considerable currency in the days of the temperance crusades' – for obvious reasons.

There are accounts ranging from those to be found in fiction (Capt Marryat's *Jacob Faithful* (1834) and Charles Dickens's *Bleak House* (1852–3)) and via those which are said to have occurred in previous centuries, to those which are said to have occurred in our own times. There is the curious case of three deaths on 7 April 1938 of John Greely, helmsman of the SS *Ulrich*; George Turner, a lorry-driver who died at Upton; and William ten Bruik who burned to death at Ubbergen in Holland. It has been suggested that the solution might lie in the fact that Ulrich, Upton and Ubbergen all begin with the letter U.

Investigators of the Phenomenon invoke Photography, Probability, Poltergeists and Pi, not to mention Phlogiston, the Pull of gravity and a Professor of Pathology – though they do not mention this particular alliterative connection. I would point out, however, that the Office of Population Censuses and Surveys knows nothing of spontaneous combustion, though this ignorance is no doubt 'all part of the plot'.

Sudden or premature death somehow seems much worse than a slow, patiently-awaited departure, and what could be more sudden or unexpected than to burst into flames?

The authoritative Glaister shows us a photograph depicting 'Almost complete destruction of body with relatively slight surrounding damage. The fuel was supplied by the natural body fat,' a theory borne out by this report:

In 1938, in a boat on the Norfolk Broads, Mrs Mary Carpenter burst into flames and was reduced to ashes in full view of her husband and children. Her family – and the boat – were unharmed.

As a footnote to that particular account, the scientists are reputed to have said that 'it could be some kind of molecular or chemical disintegration, triggered by an increase in the Earth's magnetic field.' There are reports of such occurrences from time to time, and of research that shows that, once alight, a body's fire is self-sustaining. We should be thankful that it doesn't happen too often.

There has always been a recognition of the dangers of being buried alive, and there are plenty of patents for coffins with breathing tubes, communications systems and provision for supplies of food and water pending exhumation.

Emily Josephine Jepson, a lady of 'no calling', residing at Panton Cottage, Union Lane, Cambridge, was granted British patent number 26418 of 1903 for her

> Improved Coffin for Indicating the Burial Alive of a Person in a Trance or suffering from a comatose state so that same may be released or rescued, has means for admitting air to the coffin and for giving an audible signal by means of an electric bell, which may be placed either on the grave or in the cemetery house. There is a glass plate in the lid, and a small shelf attached to one side of the coffin which may hold a hammer, matches and candle so that, when the person wakes, he can light the candle and with the hammer break the glass plate, thus assisting to liberate himself when the earth above the coffin is removed.

Frankly, I would think that a face full of glass splinters and graveyard soil would be some deterrent; air polluted with matches and burning candle very little better.

A granny, aged 80, wanted desperately to be buried (when the time came) bedecked in all her jewellery. However, she had heard tales of grave robbers cutting the fingers from corpses in order to remove the rings, and in so doing, awakening them from the dead. She was so worried that the same fate would befall her that she had written into her will a last request that all her fingers should be cut before she was buried to make sure that she was properly dead. What a waste of jewellery. And fingers.

I would be very glad to report that live burial is just not on, but unfortunately there are authoritative reports which are far from reassuring:

> There have been a number of cases in recent years when people who have been examined by qualified medical practitioners, some-times in hospitals, have been transported to mortuaries where they have been found to be alive by the mortuary attendants. *This gives the profession a bad image and should be avoided.*

The italics are mine, for it is not made clear which profession is at risk. One would like to think that it's the qualified practitioner, but I fear that the implication is that attendants ought to stand by with clubs at the ready rather than drawing attention to the faulty diagnoses of their no doubt more highly-esteemed brethren

After being pronounced dead, a 75-year-old Manchester man lay on a mortuary slab for a day and a night, to be found to be alive 27 hours later. During a routine check [why?] by undertakers the man showed unmistakable signs of life. He was rushed in high hopes to North Manchester General Hospital, but a heart machine [whatever *that* might be] failed to revive him.

Still in the mortuary, one of the great forensic pathologists was (naturally enough) a frequent visitor to a certain London mortuary which was always immaculately kept by one of the old school of attendants bursting with pride at his calling. There arose between the pathologist and the attendant that brand of friendship that cements two such men of relative standing – officer and batman, tycoon and chauffeur, *etc.* 'Your mortuary is so clean that you could eat off the floor,' oft quipped the pathologist.

One particularly heavy day, the pathologist returned from Bristol to find a message at Paddington station calling him to an urgent case at the mortuary, so he bought some sandwiches and a pie at the buffet and took a taxi to the mortuary. He rushed in, case and umbrella in one hand; half-eaten pie in the other. The attendant came to take his coat and in the scramble the pie fell to the floor. The pathologist looked at the attendant, and the attendant looked at the pathologist. The pathologist gulped, and picked up the pie. 'Well,' he said, 'here goes . . . '

Death is a peculiar subject. As I remarked earlier, to have known a recently deceased person, however slightly, confers some reflected glory on us. If we knew the deceased more intimately, it takes some time to come to terms with the fact that we shall never see, nor hear, that person again. Some never come to terms with the fact, and are useful fodder for some mediums and purveyors of religion. Not all, though. I doubt if anyone would dispute that the roots of primitive religion lie in the mysticism of death. We have neither the room nor the brief to explore such thoughts here, but the following quotation brings us back to the myth, and demonstrates once again the Pelion–Ossa syndrome – the more a person's statement is questioned, the more are they likely to wind themselves deeper and deeper into the mud of unjustified – and unjustifiable – defence.

That the human body changes weight at the moment of death is believed by great numbers of people who, however, divide themselves into opposing camps – the lighter-weights and the heavier-weights. According to Bergen Evans:

> Those who believe that the body becomes lighter seem to think that the soul has weight, weight that must of necessity depart with it, and – with that brisk disregard for strict veracity which so frequently marks discussions of this nature – have claimed that dying men, at the very moment of their decease, have been placed on delicate scales that have recorded their mortuary degravitation. But these persons have never been able to specify in just what ghoulish laboratory this took place, or what private home was so interestingly equipped, or the names and addresses of the relatives who so commendably placed scientific and religious curiosity before sentimental concern for the patient's comfort . . .
>
> More prevalent is the other belief, expressed in the phrase 'dead weight', that a body weighs more after death. But it only *seems* to weigh more . . .

But now there is hope:

> Dr Nils-Olof Jacobson, an enquiring Swede, believes he can weigh the human soul. Placing hospital beds on sensitive scales, he finds that at the precise moment of death they register a decrease of about eight-tenths of an ounce.

So there's your ghoulish laboratory. Note that the scales need to be accurate to something of the order of one part in 50,000 and ask yourself how 'the precise moment of death' is determined without upsetting the instant measurement – although it is, of course, possible that the change in weight is taken as signalling the precise moment – another example of cause and effect not perhaps being all they seem.

At the time of the emergence of the pill, there were numerous stories of daughters removing their mothers' pills for their own use, and substituting something similar in appearance. Presumably this was before the days of the bubble-pack. The mother, of course, became pregnant, and the daughter didn't.

There are tales of precocious little children who, desirous of the company of a little sibling, pierce the French letter pack with a needle, an attack which of course passes unnoticed in the heat of the moment of use.

A friend asked a teenage neighbour if she would babysit for her that evening. The young lady said yes, and would it be OK for her boyfriend to come round and keep her company. The friend readily acquiesced and went out. However, a change of plan brought her back much earlier than expected, and she arrived home to find the couple energetically engaged in the bedroom. The young man beat a hasty retreat. The friend decided that, rather than lecture the abandoned girl, she would offer some maternal advice . . . particularly as the babysitter was only 15 years old. Skilfully, she brought the subject round to contraception; had they in fact used anything and, if so, what? 'Oh yes,' said the girl, brimming with all the confidence of a TV advertisement, 'we always use Cling-film and a rubber band.'

A foaf's sister shares a flat with two other girls. She told of their inebriated return one night, with three young men. Her older sharer – more experienced – asked the younger if she'd like a contraceptive device, an offer eagerly accepted. In the morning, the donee was asked how she got on with it. 'All right,' she said, 'except that it tasted horrible.'

This puts one in mind of the newly-qualified lad who issued an unsophisticate with some suppositories, instructing him to insert one in the rectum each morning and evening.

When the patient returned it was clear that he hadn't followed the instructions – 'Have you been inserting them in your rectum?' 'Course I 'ave Doctor. What d'you expect me to do, stick 'em up me bum?'

A friend of mine when young was completely nonplussed when the doctor handed him an ice-cream carton, saying: 'Make me a stool.' There is no virtue in obscurity for the sake of delicacy.

We should now spend some time considering more far-fetched myths of sterility, impregnation, telegony and parturition.

Sterility, caused by agents at a distance using secret means, is unpleasant to contemplate and difficult to prove or disprove. It was officially stated that the Russians had *not* been using beams of microwave energy to sterilise the inhabitants of the American Embassy. But whoever thought that they had been? My guess is that if radio and television were not (on balance) a boon and a blessing to men, the electromagnetic radiation (EMR) which enables them to function would be accused of causing any dread disease or condition for which a scapegoat was needed. After all, 'they' got very het up about radiation from computer screens, about which we seem to have heard little lately.

The jury is still out on the effects of EMR from power transmission and distribution systems, and the now omnipervasive mobile phones. Some years ago, a group of Young Scientists (of the Year – BBC TV) demonstrated that EMR appeared to affect the growth of plants; an experiment of the utmost importance that seems to have sunk without trace.

But since magnetometry works, it seems reasonable that, with all the EMR flying about, something may affect somebody somewhere sometime – and possibly quite a lot of bodies for a lot of the time.

And how do we know who's telling the truth? Is the Sellafield leukaemia being reassessed in the light of recent revelations? Matter discharged from Sellafield, a 'leaked confidential report' states, is carried by the seas and washed in by the tides. 'Children under 10 living within 800 metres of the sea [on allegedly affected coasts] are three times more likely to suffer a brain tumour than the average for England and Wales.' And a lot more besides.

Beware of such phrases as: 'there can be no absolutely no connection between A and B,' and 'nothing can possibly go wrong'.

Whenever adverse effects impinge upon greed the latter seems likely to win, especially if we're dealing with a public utility or a multinational conglomerate. When it's the other way round, for example the government -*v*- the farming community (*Salmonella*, BSE, *etc*) the effect can be far more dramatic.

That the skill of the chef could be endangered by the development of the frozen pre-packed meal and the microwave oven is perhaps rationalised and articulated in microwave oven myths: that they can cook your kidneys; that they make you sterile, and that chefs are issued with 'Geiger counters', to measure the dose of radiation they receive. And as soon as someone asserts that he knows someone whose kidneys have been cooked, *etc*, there's your UL.

Of course, 'cooking kidneys' can be a joke on a par with making things out of one's own head, or asking a butcher if he has any brains. But I think that there is slightly more depth in the kidneys being singled out by the death-rays for cooking. My mother averred that if you sat on radiators, you would 'melt the fat round your kidneys', backing up the story by saying that there was someone at her school to whom it actually happened. Of all the internal organs, the ones with which most people are familiar are the kidneys – they are much more defined than the amorphous liver. And of course the kidneys are associated with dialysis and transplants, and the need for kidneys to transplant being met by unsuspecting people being kidnapped when on holiday, and waking up having had a kidney stolen – 'It's well known . . . it's *always* happening!'

Again, 'kidneys' is a euphemism for 'testicles' and that, added to the urogenital (not to be confused with Eurogenital) connection, gives the kidneys a special aura of singularity, and links kidneys and sterility.

Geiger counters are, of course, for detecting radioactivity (which might make you sterile) and not microwave radiation. That particular story (chefs carrying Geiger counters) has appeared in the national press – as if chefs didn't have a hard enough life slaving over hot stoves without having to lug pieces of monitoring equipment about – who would wonder if they settled for sterility? The germ of the idea probably springs from the dosemeters which radiographers and others wear.

However, the history of insidious sterility should give us no cause for complacency. The pioneers of X-rays and radioactivity at the turn of the century had no idea what their work was doing to them until it was too late.

Perhaps it's not surprising to find that, according to Evans:

> In the summer of 1943 absenteeism among woman war workers [in the USA] reached such proportions that sabotage was suspected and agents of the FBI were called in to investigate. Their finding, confirmed by other governments and private agencies, was that women were being driven from lathes and benches by strange sexual fears. Some feared sterility from welding or from working with ultraviolet or infrared rays. Some feared that riveting caused cancer of the breast. A wholly new and fictitious female disorder – 'riveter's ovaries' – had been invented. And scores of women engaged in filling fire extinguishers for aeroplanes had left in panic when it was rumoured that the material they were handling, carbon tetrachloride, caused pregnancy.

Mind you, there's nothing to say that these rumours were not started by saboteurs. As for the last one – that CCl_4 *causes* pregnancy – what more evidence is needed for the importance of a proper sex education?

The causes of pregnancy (apart from the well-known one) are many and varied. One of the most persistent is that women have conceived after using lavatories, baths or washing equipment previously used by men. Clearly, this makes a good excuse for anything untoward which may befall an innocent maiden, and is slightly more credible than the traditional kissing a frog.

If (some) women live in fear of lurking sperm, how much more are they concerned about the possibility of giving birth to animals?

It was current along the Atlantic seaboard of America in the mid-1930s that a girl had hatched an octopus egg – presumably nurtured in her womb, presumably taken on board while bathing. And a nurse 'died in terrible agony' when a snake which she was nurturing in her stomach bit her. In this case, it appears, she had been put on a diet and the snake, annoyed by the shortage of food, had decided to eat its host. (Snake eggs, some believe, may be ingested by drinking from a garden hose. There's sympathetic magic for you!)

Snakes, again no doubt because of their shape, have oft been accused of springing from the ground and penetrating ladies – the fear becomes a mythical reality. It is interesting to note that the 'subtil serpent' of Genesis, which is now represented as curling round the apple-tree chatting matily to Eve, originally went up inside her.

Said Rabbi Jose: 'Why is it that many kinds of magic and divination are only found in women?' R Isaac replied: 'Thus I have learnt, that when the serpent had intercourse with Eve he injected defilement into her, but not into her husband.' R Jose then went up to R Isaac and kissed him [Et tu, Jose?], saying: 'many a time have I asked this question, but not until now have I received a real answer.'

This information appears in other sources, but it was too much for the editors of our present Bible, who arranged the transformation in about 500BCE.

It's one thing to nurture someone else's egg in your bosom; another to be fertilised by an animal. Mrs Joshua Tofts of Guildford was frightened by a rabbit, and gave birth to a litter of rabbits – she said. That was in 1727. Later, she admitted the deception.

Since then, the public has been regaled with tales of animal births from time to time, and almost every old-established community, it seems, has a whispered account of such an occurrence.

Whenever the husband is away for a long time – 'at the wars' for example – there is always the danger of his spouse giving birth to animals. Often, it is an officer's wife, and she gives birth to a litter of alsatian pups. The combination of officer's wife and alsatian (now German Shepherd) seems inevitable; there is, one feels, a level below which the story would fail to satisfy. Terence Rattigan catches the mood nicely in *Flare Path*. Why the mismatched chromosomes choose to represent the father wholly is unclear, putting one in mind of Magritte's witty depiction of the front end of a fish with human legs – we all want the merperson to be composed the other way round.

Presumably women who mate with animals are worried by telegony, a concept – possibly even now – as widespread as it is false. The belief is that impregnation by a particular sire can affect all future offspring, and the famous example is Lord Morton's Foal. Lord Morton produced a hybrid from a quagga stallion and a chestnut mare. (This was at the beginning of the nineteenth century, before the quagga became extinct.)

Subsequently the mare produced three foals (in three pregnancies) by a black Arabian stallion; all the foals showed 'distinct quagga-like stripes, "proving conclusively" that the germ cells of the mare had been "infected" by the quagga' for all time. It has not been possible to replicate this result (using a zebra instead of a quagga); neither is there any evidence from years of well-documented breeding of all sorts, or from physiological principles.

Even so, it used to be thought that for a woman to produce children by the dead husband's brother (if she had already children by her dead husband) was 'uneugenic'. Presumably it would not be entirely unexpected if the products of the two unions *did* bear some similarity. But why it should be uneugenic *per se*, with or without telegony, escapes me.

The production of large numbers of children is something that catches the public fancy, though 10 seems to be the absolute upper limit since reliable records began. However, before science was quite as scientific as we now believe it to be, strange events were reported from time to time such as that reported (via Ripley) on a plaque in an abbey near The Hague. In translation, it reads:

Margaret, daughter of the illustrious Lord Florent Count of Holland, and of Mathilde, daughter of Henri, Duke of Brabant, Sister of William, King of Germany, being 42 years of age, was delivered on the Friday before Easter, at 9 o'clock in the morning, in the year 1276, of 365 babies male and female which (in the presence of several great lords and gentlemen) were arranged in front of the font and were all baptised by a bishop, the males being christened the same name, namely Jean, and the females Elizabeth. All died soon after, as did the mother, and all were buried in the same sepulchre.

Probably what we call a 'hydatidiform mole' ('bunch of grapes pregnancy'), which is what happens when the chorionic villi get out of control. Doubtless the bishop and the members of the court were somewhat myopic, a condition exacerbated by the mother's being the king's niece.

The apparent opportunities for medical students to have fun in and out of the dissecting room are obvious. A widely-told story concerns a student who borrowed a set of male genitals and went out for some hilarity. After an evening's drinking, he concealed himself in a doorway with his trophy, and practised flashing, only to be interrupted by a young policeman: 'What's going on here, then?' The student dropped the parts and took to his heels. The policeman shone his torch on the ground, and went out like a light.

Some students blindfolded a friend and drew (the blunt side of) a cold steel knife across his throat while squirting warm tomato sauce down his neck and shirt. When they removed the blindfold he died of shock.

A student climbs into a window of St John's College carrying some entrails he has acquired from a butcher's shop. He places the bloody offal on the window sill spikes, lets out an awful yell, and quickly departs. It takes the resident professor of anatomy to identify that the remains are not human.

A variant for less hardy company concerns a student who borrowed a finger before setting out on a train journey. He arranged for the door of his compartment to be improperly shut, so that a porter on the platform gave it a hefty shove as the train drew past him. At that signal, the student threw the finger out of the window, uttering a suitable yell of pain. The porter is said to have fainted – presumably his cause-and-effect reasoning wasn't working too well.

If that story is an ambiguous legend/funny story, the next surely bears the stamp of the classic UL – since telling it tends to give rise to a particular sort of silence. In fact, it's a 'head-dropper' (p 37); it leaves the auditor cold, and therefore speechless, and probably looking at the ground.

Some medical students acquired a leg from the dissecting rooms and put it in a girl's bed; they then concealed themselves to enjoy the fun. The girl returned to her room, undressed and got into bed. There was no sound. Uneasily they conferred – what should they do? They decided that the best thing would be to creep slowly away, which they did. The following day, they had no need to go to the trouble of making discreet inquiries – the news was soon abroad that the girl had been found rigidly clutching the leg, staring, staring in front of her. She has not spoken since – a common phenomenon, it seems.

In most museums of pathology, there are various creatures displayed in jars. It may have been at that same medical school where some students connected electrical wires to a preserved cyclops baby so that it could be made to wink at passers-by.

In the days when women were a rarity in medical schools, a professor dissecting a penis was asked by the only female in the class: 'Where's the bone?'

Someone overheard someone, who knows a girl, whose boyfriend's sister is a nurse at Addenbrooke's Hospital (how's that for a foaf's pedigree?), explaining that this nurse had told of some foreign medical students who went into the mortuary and propped up a corpse, giving it a cup of coffee to hold. When the porter went to collect the body, he fainted, and was last seen being carted out on a stretcher.

A story that became rife in the seventies concerned a woman who went to the doctor with a pain in her face. The doctor examined her, and asked her to remove her dentures. Under the upper plate was

COR! FOR A MINUTE THERE I THOUGHT IT WAS ONE OF MINE!

lodged a tomato pip, which had germinated, and whose roots were 'several inches' into the gum – and growing round into the brain, presumably.

A friend was accosted by an elderly porter at a country station while she was waiting for a train – a very difficult situation from which to escape. He explained to her in great detail the horrors of eating tomatoes, for the pips germinate inside you and give you cancer. Goose-berry pips – and, I'm told, apple pips – collect in your appendix and give you appendicitis.

A friend's next door neighbour is a doctor at the John Radcliffe Hospital, and had to perform an emergency appendectomy on a female punk rocker who had dyed all her hair green, and who had tattooed on her belly: 'Keep off the grass.' However, when she regained consciousness, she discovered that the doctor had written alongside: 'Sorry, we had to mow the lawn'.

A foaf had something wrong with his neck; he walked with his head tilted very much to one side. He told people that this was because, as a child, he had had trouble with his ears. The penicillin he had been prescribed had not cured him – in fact most of it had run out and trickled down his neck.

My grandfather used to scrape the loose scales off his sardines – a tedious ritual since his pet theory was that the scales 'formed a lining on the inside of the stomach.

Some people don't like flowers on the table, 'lest the pollen should get into their food,' said I, 'and they give birth to a buttercup,' added my father.

Toward the end of a holiday in Spain, a girl received a rather nasty bite on her neck. She had planned to ask her doctor if it was serious, but when she returned home it began to heal quite nicely. A week or so later, she was drowsily sunbathing in her garden when the scab began to itch. Absent-mindedly, she scratched it, the scab fell off, and a newly hatched family of baby spiders ran down her neck.

A man and his wife were assessing the quality of a roll of carpet in a shop; the woman put her hand into the roll, shrieked and fainted. She was rushed to hospital in a critical condition and died later the same day. Naturally the carpet fell under suspicion and was taken to a safe place and carefully unrolled. Inside they found a nest of poisonous snakes which had apparently only just hatched.

When a store (usually named as Harrods – at least, in days of yore) wants to compensate 'a lady' for wrongful detention for shoplifting, the aggrieved party is offered 'anything from stock'. In such a situation, she chooses a Steinway grand. But even this will not compensate for death by snakebite.

A man at Aberdeen University spent his entire student grant within a fortnight. In order to keep himself alive for the rest of the term he cooked as much porridge as he could, lined a chest of drawers with greaseproof paper and poured in the porridge to set. Every time he needed a meal he would cut off a chunk, fry it, and eat it. He found this spend-then-diet routine most satisfactory and repeated it term after term. At the end of his third year he was admitted to hospital as Aberdeen's first recorded case of scurvy in 120 years.

Sydney Garfield said that he was told the following story by a dentist who wished to remain anonymous – he calls him Dr Firenzi. Dr Firenzi was asked by a patient called Steve Pulaski:

'Could you extract a tooth for my mother? She has a terrible toothache.'

'Of course,' Dr Firenzi replied, 'Bring her to my office whenever you like.'

'That's impossible, my mother is paralysed and can't move.'

Steve offered to pick up Dr Firenzi Saturday noon; they went up to Steve's mother's flat. She was stout, about sixty-six years old, sitting immobile in an overstuffed chair, head rigidly fixed, staring wide blank eyed . . . Dr Firenzi soon saw that long neglect demanded that not only should the seemingly single pain-causing tooth be removed, but all the rest as well.

Carefully, Steve holding the flashlight, Dr Firenzi cleaned the area, applied anaesthetics and medications, and extracted the tooth. Healing was satisfactory. Every Saturday, guarding against infection, Dr Firenzi cautiously removed another tooth. On his third visit, he was amazed when Mrs Pulaski directed his attention to the fact that she could move the fingers of her left hand. With these fingers she gestured towards her extracted teeth. And regularly, each week, as if by magic, as each additional tooth was removed, Mrs Pulaski found that she could move another part of her body until she was back to her old self.

She was born again . . .

This case is exceptional . . .

A man, reportedly a homosexual, was taken to the casualty ward of a hospital with a small pineapple juice bottle inextricably inserted. The doctor, whom the teller averred was his father, could not think how to pull it out without breaking it, but at last inspiration came. He inserted a length of corkscrewed coat-hanger wire in the bottle, filled it with plaster of Paris, let it set, and was then able to pull out the bottle. As he did so, the young, naïve student nurse at his side asked: 'However did he swallow it in the first place?'

It may have been at the same hospital where a young man of like persuasion minced painfully into the casualty department and confided that he 'seemed to have sat on something'. On examination, the 'something' turned out to be a length of stiff, thick-walled rubber tubing, which was stuck fast. An operation was needed to remove it 'and, do you know, they were actually selling tickets for the operating theatre? A local anaesthetic was used and it was the patient himself who enjoyed the proceedings most of all!'

Talking of back passages, it was during my national service attachment to a military hospital that I first heard about a patient in the officers' wing: a national service second lieutenant who was as unpleasant as some national service second lieutenants could be. What's more, he was much less seriously ill than many of the other patients, whom he managed to upset considerably. One day, a walking patient from the other officers' ward put on a white coat and approached the dozing offender. He grabbed the patient's chart from the end of the bed and affected to study it. Then he turned to the patient.

'Good morning,' he said, in a curt tone which brooked no nonsense. 'Turn on your face and pull down your trousers. I'd like to take your rectal temperature.'

The patient had no second thoughts – they had clearly understood the seriousness of his condition at last, and sent this visiting specialist. He turned on his face, and pulled down his pyjama trousers. Much to everyone's delight, the 'visiting specialist' inserted a greased daffodil in the officer's orifice and slipped silently away.

4

Rich and Famous

How are you? How are you? I r'member your face, but
I can't put a name to it.
                              Hippy Damer to Queen Victoria

I have long held a theory, borne out by the telecoverage of jubilee
walkabouts, that the Royal Family must think that 'the people' are a
happy lot, just as everywhere – to them – smells of fresh paint. The
reason is that the aura surrounding royals is such that it makes people
smile, stretch forth their arms to touch (shades of the King's Evil),
and utter banalities which become pearls of wisdom.

There are, of course, those who grudge the Royal Family everything they have, and they it is, no doubt, who tell us with satisfaction
that such and such member of it is mentally underprivileged, if not
actually suffering from Down's syndrome (which presumably does
not exhibit its usual manifestations on royal visages). In 1977, Paul
Ferris suggested:

> Radio reporters at jubilees should be restrained from asking
> citizens: 'Where have you come from to day?' This was one of the
> two questions that kept hitting microphones with a dull clunk last
> week. The other was: 'What did the Queen/Prince Philip say to
> you?' The answer to this, as often as not, was: 'Where have you
> come from today?'

A foaf who knows an under-footman at Buckingham Palace tells of
the secret forays which the Queen makes late at night, emerging
from a side door of Buckingham Palace and window-shopping in
Piccadilly, Bond Street, Oxford Street and that area.

The Sultan of Turkey has a ready and kindly wit, which has served
him well on occasion. Once, when he was walking through the
outskirts of Constantinople, he noticed some men at work on the
road. It was a hot afternoon, and he remarked to the nearest:
'Warm work, eh?' The workman laughingly assented.

The purpose of including this wenge little story is to set the record straight. It was published in the early 1970s, as an example of the ready and kindly wit of a certain king:

(. . . 'Hot work,' quipped his affable majesty. The workman laughingly assented.) Then I found the version quoted above in one of the volumes (*Brave Old World* (1936)) that I keep in the necessary-house for following Lord Chesterfield's advice. You'll recognise the tale when it turns up again.

The undergraduate sees the dons filing in from the Senior Combination Room to take their places at High Table; wonders what deep philosophical matters engage them in such deep and earnest conversation. In due time, all is revealed – the weighty matters concern rhubarb and custard, and whether the mashed potato will be lumpy again.

When the lowly meet the great what is said is of little importance – it's the fact that it's said at all. The following may be the origin of a UL, or it may itself be one.

Franklin D Roosevelt never backed away from a good practical joke and, in fact, thought up quite a few himself. Once he read that people at social functions pay no attention whatever to the murmured words that are required under given circumstances. A famous hostess, for example, bidding her guests goodbye after a party, had said to each of them, with a smile on her face: 'It was a terrible thing for you to have come. I do hope you never come again.' And the departing guests, each busy framing his own proper retort, had not even noticed what she was saying.

Mr Roosevelt decided to test the thing. He chose a big White House party, where the reception line was half a mile long. As each guest came up and took his hand, the President flashed his celebrated smile and murmured: 'I murdered my grandmother this morning.'

According to the popular story, not a single guest was conscious of what he said. One former associate of Mr Roosevelt, however, denies it. He said a certain Wall Street banker was in that reception line, arrived in front of the President and heard the words: 'I murdered my grandmother this morning.' The Wall Street man then said: 'She certainly had it coming', and passed on.

If more evidence of the aura of the great be needed, I came across a study wherein people were asked to estimate the heights of the famous, and everyone accredited them with more stature than they possessed in reality. Thus it is that their feats of observation, memory and endurance are reputedly greater than those of ordinary mortals. That great men manage with far less sleep than the rest of us is often heard.

Some supermen don't wait to have it claimed for them, but advance the claim themselves. John Wesley said that he found five hours completely restful. Napoleon boasted that four were enough for him, and Edison professed to get on with even less.

But the common man would do well to save his admiration for other aspects of these heroes' careers. They were all colossal egoists who affected singularity, and whose word, in this one respect, is open to question. Wesley's greatness did not lie in the field of scientific observation; he was a firm believer in ghosts, poltergeists and witches. Napoleon so wore himself out bragging every morning how little he had slept the night before that he usually dozed off in the afternoon. Indeed, in this particular, it is a matter of satisfaction to remember that he fell asleep during a most critical period of the Battle of Waterloo, while Wellington, who professed no superhuman powers of sleeplessness, remained wide awake. And Harvey Firestone, who knew Edison as well as any man then living, said that he had a good laugh every time he heard how little Edison slept.

To be sure, the Wizard of Menlo Park allowed himself only a comparatively short period for sleep at night, but he took catnaps throughout the day which brought his total to the average.

Anyone who is 'great' may be invested with this aura of insomnia – you name them; they're sleepless. The number of reports received about the sleeplessness of its key men may be a measure of the state of a nation. A sleeping Edison tale:

One night, the inventor and his assistants laboured until 3am. Then the work was interrupted while a breakfast of ham and eggs was served. As the food was being brought in, Mr Edison fell asleep at the table. The others quickly removed his plate of ham and eggs from in front of him and substituted a plate with a few crumbs and scraps of food on it. In a few moments, Mr Edison awoke. He glanced down at the empty plate, patted his stomach with satisfaction, burped lightly, and said 'Well, let's go, boys!'

I wonder who was kidding whom?

One of the most ludicrous of the many indications of superhuman powers of the leader that are advanced by sycophantic admirers is that he can 'wear out' a dozen secretaries and whole cadres of assistants. In the telling, it is implied that the Great One pits himself against a horde of subordinates and vanquishes them – thinks more thoughts than they can comprehend, dictates more than they can transcribe, and exudes more energy than they can cope with.

This, of course, is sheer nonsense. The really great men of the world have produced their thoughts without one millionth of the clatter with which empty men conceal their total lack of thought. Plato, St Paul, Shakespeare, Newton and Einstein together, in their whole lives, probably didn't use half as much secretarial assistance as a fourth vice-president needs on an off-day. Anyone of a fussy and self-important nature who has power over others and can compel them to suit their time to his whims can wear them out, but his doing so is a mark of greatness only in his own estimation.

C Northcote Parkinson has suggested that an office-staff of 1000 people is of sufficient size to occupy itself full time with sending and receiving inter-departmental memos. In my own experience, the obfuscating output of a man who dictates woolly rubbish to his secretary (who can't spell or write English either) is responsible for much of the time wasted in this great country of ours. I have seen more than one body of enormous self-importance, who has explained how he cannot possibly live without a secretary and then, when he at last achieves the status symbol, proceed to bore the poor girl to tears. Other secretaries, of course, claim to run the office, or the great man. Those who do, don't tell you about it.

In the days when the bellows of church organs were pumped by hand there was a story of a muscular rustic who boasted that he had pumped a tune which a visiting musician had been unable to play.

What about the powers of observation of the great?

Superman can read 'at sight', can 'grasp the meaning', of an entire page, or even of an entire book, by 'photographing' it with a glance. The standard version of the myth is often assigned to Theodore Roosevelt; a friend brings him a book, and asks him his opinion of it. The President accepts the book and seems to be fingering it idly while they chat for a few minutes. The friend, on taking his leave, says that he will be interested to know Mr Roosevelt's estimate of the book when he has read it. 'I have read it,' says Mr Roosevelt (who, by the way, has been retarded as a reader when a child because of poor eyesight) 'while we were talking.' And sure enough, to his visitor's amazement, he shows a detailed knowledge of the book!

The possession of this talent has been applied to almost every distinguished figure in the modern world except Helen Keller . . .

When superman is not reading a book by flicking through the pages, he saves time by 'expert skipping,' whatever that is. 'How,' we are asked, 'does the expert skipper know what to skip without reading it first . . . One must not mistake expert skipping for skipping by an expert. If one has some knowledge of a subject it is possible to assess a book on that subject by looking at the index, and then reading on select topics. This can be done in a few moments. And surely we all have a selection of pet words which we use to test dictionaries (elychnious eutrapely), or specifics to look up in the indexes of books of whose subject we have some knowledge?

In the case of Roosevelt above, the aura of the great ensures that he gives the impression of detailed knowledge. I like to think that I'd not have let him get away with it.

Great men also have wonderful memories – or so it is said. Certainly a man's name is a precious thing, not to be trifled with, and if you are *expected* to know it, great will be the shame and the humiliation of you don't. So it is that the troops often believe that their commander knows every one of them by name: this is just one of the ways in which he gains their respect. Of course, if like the general he says cheerily: 'Good morning, good morning!' it is quite reasonable for Harry and Jack to believe that he actually knows them. And who is going to step forward, salute smartly and ask: 'What's my name, Sir?'

Here is a story which (if true) demonstrates the phenomenal memory of Disraeli. Dizzy quoted Gladstone in the House, whereupon the Grand Old Man jumped up angrily, shouting: 'I never said that in my life!' Disraeli stood stock still for three minutes; then spoke the whole of Gladstone's speech which contained the offending phrase.

From the higher echelon of the services, public and military, to those of academe. Every community has its tramps and drunks, and there is often a story attached to certain individuals that they 'were once university professors' (though this may happen only in university towns, and be believed and promulgated only by those who would derive pleasure from seeing the holders of chairs in reduced and pathetic circumstances).

After the Hungarian uprising of 1956 when large numbers of refugees arrived in this country, I heard of a factory that took many of them on to its payroll. The story was soon abroad that so and so had been a cabinet minister, another a professor and so on. Since none of them could speak English, there was no way of checking. That is probably why none of them was an artist or a musician.

Many years ago, there approached Cambridge from the North a couple who became known as The Parcels People. They had piles and piles of parcels, which seemed ever to grow. They spent the day moving the collection along the verge, and the night under polythene sheeting which protected the parcels and themselves. The route they would take, who they were, and why they were thus behaving was the subject of wide speculation, but was never revealed. There were tales of a large car (Bentley or Rolls-Royce, of course) arriving in the dead of night and its occupants providing The Parcels People with nourishment. At last, they had a fire in their parcels, which turned out to be largely old newspapers, and disappeared.

But they were not forgotten. One account later suggested that The Parcels People were none other than Rita Bandaranaike Obeyesekera and her adopted son.

The story was told that they went into a fish and chip café near Stamford and proffered a cheque in payment, which the owner refused to accept. The Parcels People then told the café owner to ring a certain number in London, which he did, and the voice at the other end of the line told the owner that the cheque would be honoured as the people concerned were very wealthy.

Unfortunately, we are not told whether or not he accepted the advice – and, of course, it was before cheques had the account-holder's name printed on them.

It was in the thirteenth century that the news of the Wandering Jew, who was supposed to have taunted Jesus on the way to the crucifixion and had been told by Him to 'go on forever till I return', first reached Europe. In 1228 an Armenian Archbishop, who was visiting St Albans in England, reported that this character, Joseph Cartaphilus by name, lived and was widely renowned in the Orient; and in 1252 this statement was confirmed by other Armenian pilgrims to the same monastery, This information was promptly recognised and hailed as a most weighty proof of Christianity, and continental writers did not fail to apply its full apologetic force against Jews and heretics. Stories of his odd experience multiplied. In most of the accounts the Wandering Jew had forsaken his false faith and adopted the true faith of Jesus, in contrast to the obduracy of his fellow Jews; several versions however have him remain a Jew, refusing to acknowledge through baptism the truth to which his own unique career testified, and thus typifying the attitude of all Jews.

Perhaps the Parcels People were the Wandering Jew in modern dress.

When it was decided to tidy up the basement of the old Zoology Department at Cambridge, there were found to be heaps of old bones belonging to nothing in particular. The local rag-and-bone man was summoned and given ten shillings to load his cart. As his horse clip-clopped down Pembroke Street, he was arrested by a wild shout: 'Hey, stop!' A dishevelled figure, waving his umbrella, stepped out into the roadway and climbed on to the cart, examining the bones, making little grunts of satisfaction. 'I'll give you a guinea for these, my man,' said the Professor of Zoology, 'if you'll just turn round and take them up the road for me.'

Many stories with a similar ring are told of the collection of scrap metal for the war effort. Railings were cut down and dumped; it was supposed to make people feel good, but when their contributions were left to rust in the area – as our Cambridge ones definitely were – their attitude turned somewhat sour.

Queen Mary did rather well. Based at Sandringham, she would tour the Norfolk lanes with a vehicle, pointing her umbrella imperiously at ploughs, harrows, tractors and so on. Apparently the technique was to collect them without question, and then to go round later and redistribute them.

A foaf is a physical chemist, and he sent a learned paper to a learned journal: in due time it was accepted and he received the proofs for correction. His argument depended on the angle of optical rotation α, and all through his paper, wherever α should have appeared, there was a tiny speck. Puzzled, he took a magnifying glass, and looked at the speck; it turned out to be a minute α ($_\alpha$). Suddenly he twigged – the last line of the paper was missing; apparently the printer had taken it as an instruction. And what was the last line? 'It will be seen, therefore, that α should be made as small as possible.'

A mathematician foaf attended an international conference at Geneva (where else?). One of the 'papers' was given by a bespectacled youth who stepped confidently forward and wrote a single-line proof of a theorem, with which students of the theory of numbers had been grappling for years, on the board. The rest of the time allocated for his paper was taken up with a standing ovation. Shades of Fermat's Last Theorem.

Sometimes extreme erudition seems to be unnecessary for securing reward. According to a friend, a man in the USA was awarded a Master's degree for sitting in a cupboard for three days. And another foaf was awarded a first class honours degree in philosophy for answering one of the questions: 'Is this a fair question?' That was all.

Have you noticed, by the way, how people always get *first class* honours degrees? You either read an 'ordinary' course or you read an 'honours' course. Honours is graded 1, 2.1, 2.2, 3 (until such time as the system levels everyone into a mush). As people always appear to get 'first class' honours, so are the sons of proud parents always 'managers' of something. And academic suicides (or any young academic who dies) are always 'brilliant'.

In Cambridge, our stories are usually of 'Oxford dons in the quad'; in Oxford, presumably, they are of 'Cambridge dons in the court.'

So, an Oxford don greeted an old student in the quad: 'Ah, Wilkinson was it you or your brother who was killed in the war?'

This was doubtless the same Oxford don who stopped to discuss some weighty matter in the quad and then, when the discussion was over asked: 'Now, which way was I going when we met?'

But we should consider awarding the palm to two Russian Grand-masters who sat opposite one another at the chessboard for thirteen hours, until at last one of them exclaimed: 'My God! Is it my move?'

I must confess that, as I advance in years, I know better how they must have felt.

A number of special tales attach themselves to the wives of professors. One, for example, was famed both for her wealth, and for the exquisite meanness of her dinner-parties, at which there would be a carefully calculated allowance of one sausage per guest. And her standard line as she served each guest the solitary delicacy was: 'Dooh let me know if you haven't got a sausage – some of my friends tell me I cheat.'

Other lines ascribed to professors' wives are: 'What a pretty tie . . . it just matches your eyes'. On entering a house lovingly restored by the architect husband of the recipient: 'It's amazing what you can do with these poky little houses'. And, the conversation having turned to cephalopods in general and octopuses in particular: 'I can't imagine what it would be like to be embraced by a beast with eight testicles'.

Dr John Campbell (1708–75) looking into a pamphlet at a book-seller's shop liked it so well as to purchase it; it was not until he had read half through that he discovered it to be of his own composition. (I know how he feels, too.)

And so to the arts. Was it the pianist Arthur Rubinstein who was asked how long he practised each day? And did he reply: 'I don't practise at all. If I don't know the music now, I never will'?

Perhaps. But we all know that recording techniques are now at such a stage of development that a work can be produced without flaw by careful editing. Is it a vile calumny on the name of a world-famous musician that he is so temperamental, and such a perfectionist, that his recordings are carefully pieced together by engineers, bar by bar? Anyone who has seen and heard him will know that this is absolute rubbish. I will not name him; if I do, I will certainly be told sooner or later that what I say is true.

James McNeill Whistler was asked by a wealthy woman to authenticate a painting: he had to do so in a court of law, went into the witness box and answered one question. Afterwards:

> Lady: How much do I owe you?
> JMcNW: One thousand dollars.
> Lady: Why, you don't mean to charge a thousand dollars for a minute's work?
> JMcNW: Not at all, I charge a thousand dollars for the labours of a lifetime.

This story bears a remarkable resemblance to an incident in the celebrated Ruskin *v* Whistler libel case. Discussing a nocturne (a Whistler night scene), counsel observed that '200 guineas was a stiffish price', and questioned Whistler on how long it took him to paint. Eventually, they agreed that it took perhaps two days, one for the main painting, and the second for finishing off.

> Counsel: Do you mean to say that you ask 200 guineas for the labour of two days???
> Whistler: No, I ask it for the labour of a lifetime.

Since this is in the court records, it is more likely to be the true version.

Both bear a similarity to the story of a plumber who submitted a bill for half a guinea for changing a tap washer. When asked how he made up this exorbitant charge he replied: 'Parts and labour, sixpence; knowing how, ten bob.'

An enthusiastic admirer of Tennyson accompanied him on an afternoon stroll round and round the terrace at Aldworth, She remained silent, lest she should stifle some priceless utterance. At last the

Great Man said: 'Coals are very dear,' and his companion, having no ready answer, was silent still. On the next circuit, he said: 'I get all my meat from London'. There was no answer to that either. Third time round he stopped by some drooping carnations. She waited with bated breath – some immortal comment on the passing of the beauty of the blooms? 'It's these cursed rabbits!' he said. That was their afternoon's conversation.

The point about great men is that they ought to be able to touch us because they have mundane thoughts, and eat, drink, sleep, *etc*, like everyone else. And yet they are expected to be perpetually intense; no doubt some of them are, but that spoils it for the others. I remember an hilarious evening spent looking at Siegfried Sassoon's irreverent collages in art annuals. Please don't forbid great men a sense of humour nor expect continual intenseness.

To deny an expert human feelings is as great a mistake as to expect him to be able to pronounce authoritatively on any field, allied or not to his own. There is no telegony of knowledge. The great writer is not necessarily a great speaker, and *vice versa*, as many commissioners of work have found to their cost.

And the less we know of a compartment of knowledge, the more hazy its boundaries. To the uninitiated, engineers, scientists and technologists are all the same though, fortunately, we don't expect a doctor of medicine to be able to treat the guinea pig . . . although . . .

Of course, there's always the possibility that the Great Man would like to talk about something other than his own speciality. Stephen Potter, an expert on S T Coleridge, made the point:

> The man who depended on mugging up the subjects of his weekend fellow guest never went very far. On one occasion, for instance, hearing that Dr Lowes, the expert on Coleridge, was to be present during a weekend holiday, [Protheroe] spent the previous month (he was a very slow reader) trying to memorise the facts of a small, mass-produced life of S T Coleridge printed in the *These Men Have Made Their Mark* series.
>
> By the Sunday evening, when the visit was coming to an end, he realised only too well that as yet no reference to Coleridge had been made. During a pause in the conversation, he decided to speak.

Protheroe: I am right in saying, I believe, that there are two versions of the 'Ancient Mariner', and they are not the same.

Lowes: 1798 and 1800?

Protheroe: 1798 and 1800 . . .

Lowes: Yes – they are not the same.

Protheroe: Not the same.

And here the conversation ended.

Perhaps we can all sympathise with Protheroe. Unless I know my company, I am loath to bore them with small-talk. I once sat through the President's tea-party at Queens', unable to think of anything which I thought anyone would think worth saying. At last, I asked him some question about a long-case clock in the Gallery. He didn't know the answer, and that was that.

Although the good Lord Chesterfield (1643–1773) may have refrained from naming the gentleman in the following story on the grounds of delicacy, I somehow doubt it. In a letter to his son, he wrote:

> I knew a gentleman who was so good a manager of his time that he would not even lose that small portion of it which the calls of nature obliged him to pass in the necessary-house; but gradually went through all the Latin poets in those moments. He bought, for example, a common edition of Horace, of which he tore off gradually a couple of pages, carried them with him to that necessary place, read them first and then sent them down as a sacrifice to Cloacina; this was so much time fairly gained, and I recommend you to follow his example . . .
>
> Books of science and of a grave sort must be read with continuity; but there are very many, and even very useful ones, which may be read with advantage by snatches and unconnectedly: such are all the good Latin poets, except Virgil in his Aeneid, and such are most of the modern poets, in which you will find many pieces worth reading that will not take above seven or eight minutes.

The great and famous (two characteristics which are by no means synonymous, especially since the explosion of the media) are well known to be tremendously mean. Sir Humphrey Mynors told me that he was approached at the station by Paul Getty who suggested that they share a taxi 'to save money'. Well, why not? They were next-door neighbours in Surrey.

In this conversation, someone will sooner or later say that it's only by behaving like this that the rich become rich. And then someone will bring in Paul Getty's coin boxes, and Gulbenkian's using a London taxi 'which will turn on a sixpence, whatever that is'.

And everyone knows of the local television celebrity who looks so cheerful on the screen, with his dispensations of largesse, the ideal man to open the village fete. But they couldn't afford the £500 fee he demanded for the privilege . . .

It is well known that all judges (and policemen) are freemasons, but what a strangely ambivalent brotherhood, for so, by all accounts, are all notorious murderers.

The story was told of Christie (10 Rillington Place), Haigh (Acid bath), Hume (Stanley Setty), and practically everyone else (except Ruth Ellis) that when he stood in the dock for sentence, and the Judge's Clerk placed the 'black cap' on the judge's head, the murderer made a Masonic Sign. This was acknowledged by the judge 'but it was far too late for him to do anything about it'.

(By the way, if a black cap for a death sentence, why not a white one for a life sentence?)

One of the ways of becoming the subject of a UL is to be either specially good or bad. The good become better; the bad become worse.

I will leave questions such as whether or not Christianity was really invented by St Paul, and merely point out that the leader of any movement tends to fulfil prophesies, and accrete legends of his fitness of purpose, in much the same way as Nostradamus and Mother Shipton have been credited with feats not theirs in order to spuriously increase their stature. Moreover, the movement will accrete unto itself elements of the mores of the people it serves, to gain acceptance. However, I'm not discussing this.

Instead, let us look at the Russian monk Grigori Yefimovitch Rasputin. Born about 1869, he lived quietly in his native village until 1904, when he became notorious for his extravagant teachings – almost Messianic, save that he advocated sin in order to obtain repentance and salvation. This was clearly likely to attract a following: if people are going to sin, they might as well have the guilt taken out of it.

Rasputin was presented at the Russian court in 1907, and when he (supposedly) improved the health of the Tsarevitch Alexis, the doctors having given up hope, it seemed a miracle – at least to the Tsar and Tsarina. After that, he was unable to do wrong and in spite, or because, of this was hated by the bulk of the nation and most of the nobility.

How he finally met his end is the subject of some conjecture, but it is generally 'known' that he had some secret power of immortality, and that he had to be 'killed' many times before he would die.

The deed was carried out by Prince Yousopov and friends. Yousopov prepared his properties in the basement of his palace, and persuaded Rasputin to visit him in the strictest secrecy. It is here that the accounts become difficult to disentangle.

In one, Rasputin is offered wine (liberally dosed with poison), but asks for tea. This is provided, and Rasputin then eats three pieces of chocolate cake, each containing enough hydrocyanic acid to kill an army. 'It's very sweet,' he says. Yousopov then pours him a glass of poisoned wine – he drinks it; then another. Rasputin says: 'There's a bitter taste in my mouth, give me some more wine to drink, I feel thirsty.' He drinks two more glasses of the poisoned wine. Yousopov is, as you can imagine, on tenterhooks. He goes upstairs and tells his waiting cronies what has – or hasn't happened. He takes a revolver and goes down again. Rasputin complains of a heavy head and a burning in the stomach. He drinks another glass of poisoned wine. Yousopov shoots him 'through the heart'; Dr Lasovert comes down and pronounces him dead.

Somehow, the enormity of what they have done to the monarch's favourite sinks in, and their only thought is to get rid of the body. They discuss this, and then Yousopov shakes Rasputin the latter opens his eyes, stands up foaming at the mouth, and crawls up the steps from the basement, making his way to the outside world. Purishkevitch shoots him four times and stamps on his face. Yousopov belabours Rasputin with a rubber truncheon until he (Yousopov!) becomes limp and loses consciousness.

Every time one hears a bar-room reconstruction of the murder, something new seems to have been added to the sequence of events – to make Rasputin seem that much more evil. So he is bashed with candlesticks, thrown out of windows, and still comes back for more – it's like Tom and Jerry – or even Itchy and Scratchy.

Another account says that Rasputin ate biscuits, not cake; Maria Rasputin – his daughter – says that her father never ate cake. No poison was found in the body.

A third account speaks of 'cakes' rather than 'pieces of cake' but again points out that Rasputin never ate cake. However, having waved the plate away, he changed his mind, and ate two. Here, Maria is reported as saying: 'I'm positive that my father did not eat the poisoned cakes, for he had a horror of sweet things.' As for the wine, she said: 'Doubtless the poison had not dissolved.' Careless.

However, she goes on to put her finger on the spot:

I am convinced that certain details given by the assassins were added partly to make the story more picturesque and partly to excuse the slaughter; for since it was a question of doing away with a being whose devilish vitality resisted cyanide, it would be understandable that the five conspirators, in their terror, should riddle him with bullets.

In this account, by the way, Yousopov does not become senseless through his exertions with the truncheon, but goes to speak to the policeman who comes to see what is going on. Nevertheless, 'going back to the dead body after the policeman had left he found that Rasputin had changed his position.'

Recently, the 1916 Bolshevik file of Rasputin has come to light. It suggests that the story of Rasputin's indestructibility was put about by Yousopov and his cronies to cover their ineptitude. The poison was diluted to homeopathic concentrations; the revolver shots missed their target. Rasputin met his end trussed up and thrown under the ice in the River Neva.

Well, there we are. I'm in danger of concluding merely what we all know – that historical research is very difficult, and you have to state what you believe to be the most likely to be true, based on the evidence available to you at the time. There is also the problem that, however well versed an historian may be in his subject, it is impossible to clear one's mind of everything that one knows that was not known until after the date of interest.

Take the problem of larping, or live action replaying by present day larpers of, let us say, 'Roman Times'. The difficulty – the impossibility – is twofold; first, we need to shed all the knowledge *we* have that the Romans didn't, knowledge that must get in the way of our trying to enter the Roman mind, and second, we need to take on board what might have been in that Roman mind – a random recall being a whole selection of gods with different responsibilities, personal lares et penates, the practise of haruspication, slaves, a calendar full of inauspicious days that works backwards, oils and strigils in the bath, all that sort of thing. And all of this, perhaps, without determining what period of Roman history we are considering – between the legendary foundation by Romulus and Remus in -753, through the establishment of the Roman Empire by the Emperor Augustus in -27, and the decline and ultimate fall in the fifth century – in total a span of more than a millennium.

Instead, of course, all Romans look alike to us. The Ancient Rome we all carry in our minds is some generalised scene with people clad in togas wandering about in a sun-kissed forum, saluting one another with arm across chest, and declaiming messages from scrolls in a stilted form of English, the whole presided over by a degenerate Emperor somewhat resembling a combination of Charles Laughton, Robert Morley and Peter Ustinov (depending on your age, and interest in the cinema) lying on a couch and being served pendulous swags of grapes and copious draughts of wine by callipygous hand-maidens, while applauding the exploits of safely-distant gladiators or hominivorous lions.

5

War and Peace

> And ye shall hear of wars and rumours of wars:
> see that ye be not troubled
>
> Matthew 24: 6

It is particularly apposite to start this chapter with a Biblical quotation, as one of the earliest ULs is to be found in the Bible (Judges 12: 5, 6):

> And the Gileadites took the passages of Jordan before the Ephraimites: and it was so, that when those Ephraimites which were escaped said Let me go over; that the men of Gilead said unto him, Art thou an Ephraimite? If he said, Nay; then said they unto him, Say now Shibboleth: for he could not frame to pronounce it right. Then they took him and slew him at the passages of Jordan: and there fell at that time of the Ephraimites forty and two thousand.'

The fear of the enemy infiltrating one's country is obviously a real and powerful one. In Holland, there is a seaside resort near The Hague called Scheveningen, and legend has it that this name, being difficult to pronounce, was used during the Second World War as a Dutch Shibboleth.

> Suspicious native (pointing to sign reading: 'Scheveningen'):
>   Read that!
> Enemy infiltrator: Scheveningen
> BANG!

The problem with Scheveningen is not so much one of getting people to say it as the fact that it is not particularly difficult to say: with a few seconds tutelage, I was able to pass muster as a Dutchman – on that one word. There are sounds in Dutch which are much more difficult for the alien to pronounce, and far less avoidable than Scheveningen; 'Ik ga' (I go) for example; Van Gogh would be another killer. If you can fool the natives with your everyday speech, specialities such as Scheveningen are child's play.

I would like to be able to report that the Dutch Bible gives the clue which links Shibboleth and Scheveningen, but it doesn't. In Denmark, spies were apparently asked to say something like 'rødgrød med fløde', a redcurrant pudding with cream.

Spies, of course, had to come down by parachute, and it was reported that they 'wore spring heels and bounced even when they jumped down from lorries.' More realistic of course, was the belief that they were equipped with bicycles so that they could move swiftly about the country.

My vivid imagination has always boggled at the thought of how one would arrange for oneself and bicycle to land safely on the same parachute.

Be that as it may, it appears that those who avoided giving an impression of the old umbrella-mender and were able to pedal away from their landing-places, were further weeded out by their forgetting to ride on the right (or left) side of the road.

The few that remained after that would be confused by the lack of direction-signs, and would inevitably have to stop and ask the way. The recommended answer to this question was 'Turn left, left, and left again.' The spy would ride off, and the direction-giver would raise a posse to await his return.

In the war that I remember, we had our own ways to identifying spies. My grandfather was annoyed by being turned down by the War Office when he offered to resume his First World War commission (after all, he was only seventy in 1939). He became quite neurotic about spies, and spent much time identifying them and their meeting places and bombarding officialdom with letters. If the country was full of old soldiers doing that, it's a wonder that the machinery didn't become quite clogged. However, G'Pa told me that if I suspected someone of being a spy, I was to accost him and ask him to say: 'Where were the wise women?' No doubt the spy would have done the honourable thing on finding that he'd been rumbled by a six-year-old, and allowed me to lead him to the nearest policeman.

As everyone knows, spies or escapers on the continent wore rough serge clothes and berets and masqueraded as dim relatives of members of the underground. In Britain, on the other hand, spies tended to be disguised as nuns.

A foaf was sitting opposite a nun on a train; she was reading the Bible, but dropped off to sleep and the book fell on the floor. She bent down to retrieve it and her habit slid up to reveal a hairy arm with a portrait of Hitler tattooed on it.

One wonders whether this story had any connection with the Father Brown story wherein Brown recognises Flambeau, the arch criminal: 'I suspected you when we first met. It's that little bulge up the sleeve where you people have the spiked bracelet. '

(I have a feeling that today the phrase 'you people' could land one in it. Wow!)

Unfortunately, once a dangerous type is identified, it may have far-reaching effects on the innocent. Perhaps nowadays it is hard to credit this nation of animal-lovers with ill-treating dachshunds just because the breed had a German name, but the state of hatred ran so high that this certainly did happen. Even the disclosure that Dachshund (German) = Brocker (Anglo-Saxon) = Badger-hound (English) failed to stop the rot.

However, even if the Brocker couldn't be disguised, his owner obviously could, and yet there were reports of men with close-cropped hair and wearing monocles – and even jack-boots – stirring up racial hatred at public meetings. Since it is incredible that a genuine enemy infiltrator would be so stupid as to continue to exhibit his stereotyping characteristics, one may perhaps assume that such stories were an oblique way of scornfully pointing out unthinking Germanic military stupidity.

So it was that there was a much-told spy rumour, wherein a tradesman called at a newly-let house to solicit custom (that dates it!) When the door was opened, he recoiled in horror, for there was the brutal Prussian who had commanded the prisoner-of-war camp in which the caller had spent the First World War.

Before France was occupied, there was a story current that the station-master at such and such a station had been discovered to be a spy. The way in which it happened was as follows. The authorities noticed that somehow the Germans always managed to bomb the station when there was a troop train there – and sometimes, it seemed, the stationmaster would even delay the train until the enemy bombers arrived.

An intelligence watch was therefore kept on the man, and one day, when there was a troop-train standing at the platform, the stationmaster's young son ran up to him and told him that he was wanted on the telephone. 'Impossible!' said the stationmaster, 'The line has been cut.' 'No,' urged the boy. 'It's the telephone in the cellar.' The intelligence man went to investigate, and heard a German voice on the other end of the secret telephone in the cellar. The spy was unmasked.

A number of ULs concerned with the war would appear to have had their bases in psychological wishes that there would be no war (the Beaverbrook syndrome), or that the war would be over by a certain date. This is hardly surprising. Underlying rational man is a seething mass of irrationality, compulsion mania, sympathetic magic and the rest. Why else should there be scarcely a paper without a horoscope?

I am sure that I was not alone in 'reasoning': the First War began in 1914 and lasted until 1918; the Second War began in 1939 and will therefore stop in 1943. That didn't work, but it was a comfort. Later, I said: 1914 to 1939 was 25 years, therefore the next war will start in 1964. Happily, that didn't work either. It is a complex game of 'she loves me, she loves me not'; we know the answer we want, and we keep picking flowers until we have a simple majority. If that doesn't work, we say 'things go by opposites'. A silence falls on the assembled company; someone is bound to say: 'it must be twenty past' and some may even 'correct' their watches! In spite of the palpable futility of their exercises, we may continue with them *ad nauseum.*

Psychoanalyst Marie Bonaparte gives a full account of several widespread myths, and examines the psychoanalytical rationale underlying them. She reports her first in twenty-nine guises; it runs as follows:

A foaf is driving along when he sees a woman by the roadside seeking a lift. He stops, and the woman turns out to be a fortune-teller, who says that before he gets home there will be a corpse in his car. She then follows this extraordinary piece of news (which he doesn't believe for one moment) with the prophecy that there will be no war (if the story is told before the war) or that the war will end on a certain date (if the story is told during the war). Other versions foretell Hitler's death, he being the force behind the war. But to return to the corpse. The fortune-teller is set down, and the traveller continues on his journey: however, either he takes on another passenger, or he calls at the house of a friend who seeks a lift for himself (or another), or he comes across a road accident and takes the victim to hospital. Whatever the detail, he takes a passenger, and the passenger dies in transit. The story, it appears, was current not only in Europe, but also England and America.

There was another type of story which connected a prediction with Hitler's death and the end of the war – 'the myth of the guessed money'. In this story, the fortune-teller by some concatenation of circumstances is able to say how much someone else in the story has on his or her person. When surprise is expressed at this correct disclosure, the fortune-teller then goes on to say: 'It's as true as that Hitler will be dead on such and such a date, and the war will end.'

The corroboration of a known fact by a demonstrably-correct prediction seems an odd way of gaining credence. But this has happened with well-known seers from Nostradamus and Mother Shipton downwards, on to whose original works have been grafted, from time to time, updatings which make the putative originator seem that much more reliable. And the more right they seem to have been in the past, the more likely their predictions are to be right. A tortuous argument. But the principle is ambiguous: we assume that because the fortune-teller was right about the money – and there's no proof that she was – then she must be right about the awaited event. (Never assume – it makes an ASS of U & ME.)

Marie Bonaparte sees in the myths of war she quotes 'traces of ancient human sacrifice, of sacrificial gifts and of continence observed as propitiation.'
She then goes on to say:

> In our succeeding myths, the terror aroused in nations by the threat of enemy aggression gives rise to another mechanism, more primitive and even more simple, by which to control anxiety: the plain denial of the enemy's menace.

Whether or not this needs any deep, primitive psychology I find it hard to say. It is firmly rooted in people that they forget the unpleasant and remember the pleasant (such as those long, hot summers of childhood), or that they don't hear what you are saying if they don't choose to (selective auditory response), or that they stuff unopened bills behind the clock on the mantelpiece and wait for them to go away (Dun's syndrome).

A story prevalent in France just before the 1939–45 War concerned an English motorist touring the continent in his Rolls-Royce. He comes up behind (*or* rounds a corner to find) a German panzer division. He cannot stop in time (*or* his brakes fail) – he closes his eyes and waits for the crash. There is indeed a crash, but when he opens his eyes he finds that his car is more or less undamaged, and the tank is in pieces – it's made of plywood and canvas. On the continent, the reciprocal story circulated: a German was touring in England in his Mercedes, and the same thing happened. But of course, there were such deceptions being carried on, so the tale may well be true, but has taken on the trappings of a legend – if only to deflect attention from the fact that if 'They' were doing it, then 'We' were no doubt doing it as well. More convolutions.

It's interesting that the cars are named as Rolls-Royce and Mercedes. These up-market makes demand well-to-do owners, which lends (spurious) credence to the tale.

Apparently this is a common trick amongst great powers. When Harold Macmillan visited Moscow in the 1960s, one of his aides somehow became detached from the touring party, and found himself able to take a closer look at the ultramodern fighters parked around the airfield. They turned out to be made of plywood. But the whole airfield might have been a sham. For did not 'We' set up whole dummy airfields with arrays of false aircraft to draw 'Their' bombs?

Much of the equipment which was wont to drive through Red Square on May Day is made of plywood. Looks good, and saves no end of money. And no doubt 'They' said the same thing about our demonstrations of might.

But the interpretation and the reality are both valid. On one hand, it's comforting to think that the armaments are a sham; that the enemy is not so fearsome after all. On the other, of course there were fake rows of fighters laid out to attract enemy attack, and divert it from the operational aircraft.

However, if 'there's a war on', and you can't imagine the enemy out of existence – nor, instantly, beat 'em – then you can try joining 'em. Stories of this genre, the friendly enemy, may have given some comfort to the fighting forces, but are not necessarily calculated to please those making their sacrifices on the home front. Reminiscences are bringing some corroboration to light; one gets the impression that 'the trenches' were some sort of maze where one might turn a corner to find oneself face to face with one's adversary. Thus they exchanged gifts at Christmas, or instantly agreed to part, each refusing to harm the other. Indeed, in some versions they are politely told that they must have taken a wrong turning, and directed back to their own lines by the 'enemy'.

Certainly the 'Christmas Truce' of 1914 is well documented; members of both sides meeting in no-man's-land, exchanging drinks, showing photos of loved ones, playing football, drawing water from the same well, and even exchanging warnings of impending attacks. And if further proof of the friendly enemy be needed, there are stories of the troops firing only when observed by their superior officers. Today, more than ever, it is suggested that troops are loth to shoot to kill, but we must wait for events to become history before we can explore that. Nobody (except a mercenary) wants to fight a war on somebody else's behalf, so there were always pacifist wiseacres suggesting that the leaders of both sides should be put 'in the ring' and left to slog it out.

It would, however, be somewhat difficult if the weaker side had the stronger leader, and vice versa. And how would the losing side feel about the result? But one agrees with the sentiment, even though it shows little regard for the complexity of the reasons for waging war. What it does show is the belief, real or wished for, that all 'ordinary people' on both sides are peace-loving beings, and all brothers under the skin.

The siege of Ladysmith during the Boer War was conducted in an unusually gentlemanly way. There was no shooting and no fighting on the Sabbath, and often the Boers took a holiday from shooting after any particularly busy day. Firing rarely began before breakfast or continued after tea, and there were regular half-hour intervals for meals.

At Christmas, some plum puddings were even provided by the Boers, who sent over shells marked 'With the Compliments of the Season' containing puddings partly cooked by the heat of the explosion in the gun barrels.

Every war produces its crop of people who are lucky to be alive, saved from the enemy missile by a pocket Bible, or a locket containing a picture of mother, over the heart. There are certain conventions: it has to be a Bible or a picture of mother: *Alice in Wonderland*, or a picture of a prize racing pigeon are excluded. And it goes without saying that the protective article has to be over the heart because in spite of all we know to the contrary, people are always shot through the heart.

Although at least some of the reality has now emerged, it is from the historical point of view of some importance to preserve the inaccuracies that went with it. The term 'Hitler's Secret Weapon' was applied equally to a particularly nauseating carrot jam and to the much more fearsome 'death ray'. The realities of wireless and the fantasies of science fiction made it easy for people to believe that our enemies were about to perfect a death ray, and no doubt our enemies believed the same about us.

There was certainly an updated story that 'We' had a secret ray which could stop the engines of cars or aircraft, and the proof of this lay in an incident which would occur, usually on a road on the South or East coast, to a foaf. He would be driving along when, all of a sudden, his engine would cut out. He would get out of the car and start to investigate the fault, when along would come the local policeman.

'Just wait a moment, sir, and it'll cure itself,' he would say, and it would. It was the defensive ray, out of hand again.

No one familiar with the Secret War of Dr R V Jones can have failed to have been amazed at the incredibly Teutonic fact that the Germans always managed to pick a code-name for their secret weapons which had some obscure mythological connection with the weapon itself, thus giving the clue to its nature – or even its very existence. Be that as it may, if you have some device, such as radar, which enables you to locate your enemy consistently better than you would be able to by chance, it must eventually dawn on him that you have such a device.

And this was the problem with radar. It is said that the rumour was deliberately spread that our pilots were fed quantities of carrots to improve their night-vision – and that this was why they were so successful in finding their targets, or avoiding enemy planes. Although carrots do contain the makings of vitamin A, which itself is essential for the production of visual purple (the pigment in the retina which enables vision in poor light), there should be enough vitamin A in the normal diet, as many foods other than carrots contain it.

Since much innocent laughter was generated by accounts of guns with curved barrels for firing round corners, it is probably well to set the record straight by quoting an authority.

The curved-barrel Maschinenpistolen were a remarkable wartime development which, however, well illustrates the gusto with which the German High Command entered into futile projects which promised relatively little and diverted valuable production time from more conventional weapons of war.

The base for the Krummlauf device was an MP44 to which was fitted a curved-barrel unit with suitable mirror sights attached to the muzzle. It has been said, though never satisfactorily proved, that, the idea was to provide a means for firing around corners without exposing the operator to hostile fire; and another version tells of the necessity for dislodging hostile Russians from tanks.

A third story, however, tells that the curved-barrel was an unexpected by-product from a project originally intended to provide a device by which firing trials could satisfactorily be accomplished without recourse to the conventional ranges; it is said that from this it was thought that other, more useful purposes could be served – and it may also be that the last tale is the most likely of the three.

However, to increase the life of the barrels, it was necessary to pierce them with holes to slow the bullet down. This in turn drastically reduced the efficiency of the gun, but they rationalised this by saying that it was 'envisaged solely as an ultra-short-range weapon' – in which case its purpose was largely negated.

On the home front, there was plenty going on, though much of it seemed to have little to do with any war which was, or was not, being fought. One of the most widespread upheavals after the departure or redeployment of the menfolk was the evacuation of thousands of children from dangerous centres to various parts of the country.

Soon there was a rich crop of 'evacuee stories'. The press offered prizes for them and the public responded by foisting off all the traditional tales about urban urchins in the country. One of the most-quoted was that of the couple who found their two billeted children lying at the extreme edges of the bed, with an empty space between. When asked why, they said, 'Well, where are youse yins going to sleep?' In another version, the children were found lying under the bed – 'this is where we always sleep at home'.

Several evacuee and other stories from this source were woven into a delightful musical *Happy as a Sandbag*. There is also a story from Sir John Hammerton:

Two East End lads billeted in a noble mansion were waiting impatiently for their breakfast. At the top of the table sat the elderly chatelaine and behind her stood the butler. When it looked as if they were going to be late for school, one of the lads said to the butler: 'When's that bloody breakfast coming?' The old lady said: 'I'm so glad you have said that. I have been wanting to say it for years.'

There were other opportunities for bravery on the home front. A foaf was firewatching during the war, when a stick of incendiary bombs came down on the town hall. He raised the alarm, and then suddenly remembered that the mayor's regalia were inside the town hall. So he dashed into the smoke and flames and found a huge and heavy chest, which he started to drag out. It was such a strain, and the smoke was so choking that several times he nearly gave up, but his civic pride spurred him on. He got the chest out, and collapsed on the steps. He woke up in hospital to find himself a hero. The chest had been full of hand-grenades and ammunition for the Home Guard. He was awarded the George Medal.

There is a military analogue of this story in *A Bridge Too Far*, where a soldier gives up his life to rescue a parachute pod of what is thought to be vital supplies, but which turns out to be – berets.

The other side of the coin showed the looting firemen. All over the country, every night, Woolworth's 3d & 6d stores were being bombed, and those who ought to have been protecting the property were in fact making off with huge quantities of ladies' underwear and stockings and selling them on the black market. (Compare the New York power failure of July 1977.)

To call into question the phenomenal accuracy of bomb-aimers is near heresy, though there is no reason to suppose that 'we' were any more accurate than 'they' until advanced methods became available.

There was, however, plenty of reason to suppose that 'they' could bomb accurately because of the current stories. And with tortuous reasoning, if 'they' were accurate, then 'we' must be as well, except that experience showed that 'they' weren't.

'Evidence' came from *The Times*, the clergy, and the air-raid wardens. In a letter to *The Times*, a First World War pilot warned that people should on no account look up at the sky when enemy aircraft were overhead, as the white blobs of numerous upturned faces could be seen from an aeroplane at a considerable height and form a good and tempting target. Those unable to contain their curiosity were advised to shade their faces with their hats.

A clergyman addressed the Chester and Warrington Methodist Synod, explaining: 'German airmen are careful not to bomb breweries and maltings in Britain because Hitler knows that if Britons go on drinking at the present rate, we shall lose the war.'

As for that well-known street-cry: 'Put out that ******* light!' ... It was a flattering tribute to the navigational powers of the Luftwaffe to suppose that it could pick out, from the heart of a darkened island, a message in code flashed from a solitary light bulb, torch or cigarette in an anonymous suburb.

ARP Wardens were necessarily unpopular at times, and the butt of an obvious UL:

A gossip writer reported that somebody had met somebody else who said that near Aldgate Pump lived a man, normally unemployed, who had been heard to boast that he had got an ARP job, that his wife and family were evacuated, and that he had never been so well off in his life, the more so as he lived rent-free – 'nobody pays rent round here, there's a war on'.

Back to the front. Two soldiers are overtaken on the road by a peasant who offers them a place in his cart. When they get in, they find a young nun already there. Further on, with nothing but open country around, she professes to be at her destination and asks to get down. Before saying goodbye, she tells the soldiers to be unafraid, that the war will end before summer, that they will suffer no hurt and that all will be well.

She then disappears and the soldiers see a piece of paper on the ground, dropped, they think, by the nun. They pick it up and deeply moved, recognise the very image of their fellow-traveller in the holy picture of St Teresa of Lisieux. Positive identification of the Angel of Mons? These days, it's done with miracle sandwiches on e-bay.

Reports of weeping effigies and pictures of female saints, not to mention the BVM, were not uncommon. Presumably it is not manly to cry, but what else can a statue do? Well, it can move, particularly if it is an assemblage of pieces. We find stories of people being 'frightened to death' by the heavy hand of a suit of armour falling on their shoulders (how is this known to be the cause of death, any more than that the whole of his life passes before the eyes of a drownee?), and Salvador Dali tells us the following:

> The story has often been told of the Andalusian anarchist who during the Civil War walked up the steps of a gutted and profaned church with the grace of a torrero, drew himself up to his full height before a crucifix whose Christ wore long natural hair, and after having insulted Him with the most atrocious blasphemies, spat into His face while with one hand he brutally seized the long hair which he was about to tear out. At this moment the Christ's hand became detached from the cross and His arm, which was articulated, fell on the shoulder of the Andalusian soldier, who dropped dead on the spot. What a believer!

It was certainly well-known that 'they put bromide in the tea/coffee' to reduce randiness, though such measures were hardly necessary in view of the strenuous régime we had to follow at the time. Such stories seem to have been prevalent everywhere and through the ages – Marie Bonaparte's 'myth of the doctored wine'. It is reported that the sexual prowess of recruits always diminished, and who can be surprised at that? In France, the wine was doctored; in Poland it was the coffee. In South Africa, it was the food itself which contained a mysterious anaphrodisiac called 'blue-stone' – as it had allegedly been in the First World War. In Germany, iodine was put into the coffee, and soda into the meat.

The story doesn't stop there:

Even more widespread is the belief that saltpetre is an anti-aphrodisiac and is secretly introduced into the food at colleges, prisons, and other places where amorous impulses are thought to have ungovernable force. It is safe to say that there is not a boys' school or an army camp in the country in which this myth is not entrenched.

As the enemy was conquered, the Royal Engineers were the first into towns and cities, in order to get the services working again. Many is the German town where a couple of sappers stayed on after the war to become the Mayor and the Chief of Police.

Many readers may have forgotten (or, more probably, never heard of) Manning Coles, creator of British Agent Tommy Hambledon. It may be to Manning Coles that we owe the story of the sappers who stayed on, or Manning Coles may have been inspired by the story.

The appropriate potted plot is as follows:

An amnesiac is fished out of the sea in January 1918 and taken to a German Naval Hospital. He is christened Klaus Lehmann (he can't remember who he really is), and starts life in Germany. In 1923 he meets Hitler, after the latter's release from prison, and through this meeting takes up a post with the National Socialist Party. Ten years later he is a deputy of the Reichstag, when the shock of the Reichstag fire suddenly brings back his memory – he is none other than Tommy Hambledon, British Intelligence Agent. As he comes to terms with his knowledge, he is offered the post of Deputy Chief of Police, which he accepts. He makes contact with London via a radio play, *The Radio Operator*, which contains coded messages in its morse background. In time, of course, he becomes Chief of Police, but his double role becomes more and more dangerous until he is forced to change clothes with a corpse with whom he can be confused. Tommy Hambledon returns to England, laughing as he hears on the wireless of the 'cowardly and brutal murder of our Chief of Police, Herr Klaus Lehmann . . . faithful servant and leader of the Reich and a trusted and beloved friend of the Führer himself, who will pronounce the oration at the State funeral on Tuesday next . . . '

In Switzerland, the following story cropped up time and again. Germans had orders to create 'incidents' in Switzerland, and cross one of the Rhine bridges and assemble in the village square. Suddenly a bugle sounds, the Germans are surrounded by Swiss soldiers and taken prisoner without a murmur. Because nothing seems to be happening, another contingent of Germans strips naked and swims across the Rhine, with their equipment in rubber bags. They are also rounded up, the bags are impounded, and they are made to parade in the nude.

Both sides of the channel had stories of pellets that would turn water into petrol. A convoy would find itself low on petrol in some deserted spot with the inevitable solitary farmhouse occupied by an old couple. They would ask for water, and fill up their tanks with it. Then they would drop in the secret pellets and, lo! The water was turned to petrol. This again seems to be a modem version of the philosopher's stone, the elixir of life, *multum in parvo*, a three-course meal in a pill. It is a pity that the secret has been lost – it would have saved all those expensive operations in the North Sea.

Unless, of course, the whole North Sea Oil boom is a myth invented by the government, aided and abetted by the media, to disguise the existence of the petrol pellets. If so, the mind-blowing level of self-consistent detail to be maintained must be similar to that required by a god setting out to create a complete and fully-functional earth in six days.

Our wartime Ministry of Information, it seems, started the rumour that we were able to set the sea on fire (using petrol pellets??) in order the prevent invasion of our island. If this information gave comfort at home, the effect it had on the enemy was devastating. The pellets would have been particularly useful on the River Thames on the night of 31 December 1999.

There were many stories of how many times the Germans had attempted to invade, and how many of them had been burnt in the blazing sea – up to 350,000 at one attempt. From there it was but a short step to tell how the Germans were committing suicide in droves, or having to be forced on board landing-craft at gunpoint, so frightened were they of being fried in the sea.

As for those who *had* been fried in the sea, the British collected the corpses identified them in some macabre sorting office, loaded them into planes, and dropped each on his home town. SPLAT, SPLAT, SPLAT! (Never mind the Rub al 'khali.)

Sometimes the MoI machinations backfired. For example, they are supposed to have disseminated a story that the Germans had invented a bomb 'which would kill 1,000,000 people and take 10,000 prisoners.' They were soon receiving desperate requests that the rumour should be denied. Apparently, the MoI had thought that the story was so silly that nobody would believe it. I cannot fathom why they would have started such a rumour in the first place.

Eventually the European war came to an end, and within three months the war in the Far East was terminated by one of the most significant events of our time – the dropping of the atomic bomb: nothing has ever been the same since. It is not surprising that the bomb gave rise to its own ULs, among them one which I remember hearing very soon after the event – that all that immense energy was contained in something the size of a matchbox. It is interesting that the same idea was current in Japan. According to a survivor:

> The bomb is the size of a matchbox. The heat of it was six thousand times that of the sun. It exploded in the air. There is some radium in it. I don't know just how it works, but when the radium is put together, it explodes.

So the war was over, but not everyone knew this. Every so often, a Japanese who hadn't heard the news was alleged to have appeared; some rejoined a society which they must have found unbearably alien; others disappeared into the jungle again, refusing to believe the news. Who can blame them? There can't be many left now.

On the other hand, there were several wanted war criminals not accounted for, and only the elapsing of their maximum life-span will assure their seekers (or their seekers' successors) that they are gone for ever.

Wanted men for obvious reasons acquire an aura of mystery, and we perhaps feel some sympathy with the one who gets away – depending upon what he's done, of course. The human emotions are complex and fickle. Ronald Biggs *et al* robbed an incomprehensible sum of money from a public body, on public transport, escaped from a penal institution and, because of the ethos surrounding that particular case (everyone having conveniently forgotten Driver Mills) became a folk hero of sorts – until, that is, he took the British Navy for a ride, an action which was just not on.

There is something romantic about a war criminal living a hard and simple life in the South American jungle – we forget why he's wanted, and even feel that he's paid for his sins many times over by his banishment.

And it may of course be something about the mysterious South America – where Colonel. Percy Fawcett disappeared, where there are strange, misunderstood artefacts of great antiquity, where there is gold to turn a man's head, and whence, some say, Jesus escaped a couple of millennia ago to start a secret sect.

In the seventies, news emerged from the South American jungle of a vast community living in luxury below the surface, heated and lit by an everlasting power source of great antiquity. The community speaks German, because some 3,000 German troops escaped there in 1941. We avidly await further news, but it would seem that the original informants have mysteriously disappeared.

6

Science and Technology

> The Church welcomes technological progress and receives it with love, for it is an indubitable fact that technological progress comes from God and, therefore, can and must lead to Him.
>
> Pope Pius XII

Technology, and matters technological, have given rise to many ULs, some of which have appeared in other chapters. A sub-set of technological stories – those pertaining to the motor car – is grouped in the next chapter.

However, a few general technological ULs of the sort you might hear while grasping a glass in one hand and a sausage on a stick in the other will not be out of place here.

A young couple (foafs, of course) purchased a house, which they wanted to modernise and decorate. They were following the instructions from a weekly partwork for knocking front and back rooms into one. They spent one Sunday morning breaking through the wall; then, tired and dusty, they went down to the local for a lunchtime drink. When they returned, they could not believe their eyes: the house had fallen down. The instalment about putting in an RSJ to support the load didn't come out until the following week.

A friend was working in a factory where there was some massive, old-fashioned machinery, which they wanted to get rid of. First, they advertised it, but no one wished to know. Then they started to take it to pieces, but the job was so slow that they calculated it would take about three months – and then there was the problem of getting rid of the parts. So eventually they swallowed their pride and sent for some machinery demolition experts.

On the appointed day came a little man with a little hammer and a big man with a big hammer. In complete silence and with a look of intense concentration on his face, the little man tapped the framework in various places; then chalked a cross at a certain spot. The big man swung his sledgehammer and, lo! the frame fractured. They carried on thus and, by lunchtime, the machinery was a heap of scrap on the floor ready for carting away.

A friend who sorted out the computer which controls one of the North Sea gas terminals programmed the machine to wish the operators 'Merry Christmas', 'Happy New Year' and so on at the appropriate time – he said. It all looks very clever, provided that the clock keeps good time. However, if it doesn't, it looks very silly. Somewhat less benign was the computer programmer whose fixed-term contract was not renewed when the time came. In a fit of pique, he programmed the software to destroy itself six months after his departure.

From such humble beginnings have sprung not only viruses, but rumours of viruses. Viruses that hide away until a certain combination of keystrokes, or a certain date, and then nibble at your software. Viruses that replicate themselves into your floppy disks, and thus infect others' machines. To combat viruses, we have virus checkers, but there are still tales of companies whose only remedy for the infection was to dispose of all their hardware and start again.

And then, of course, there was the Millennium Bug. Leaving aside the date of the True Millennium (010100 or 010101? I go for the latter) it is clear that a change from 1999 to 2000 is significant in that every digit changes. So, if anything's going to happen, that's when. Perhaps someone will tell me what experiments were done with deliberately mis-set computer dates to demonstrate the chaos. Or was it all an elaborate hoax by the computer industry to extort millions upon millions from scared technophobes?

It was fascinating to see/hear media commentators thrashing about, trying to find just one teensy weensy example of the Millennium Bug's striking. In my recollection, all we had was a *rumour* that a Japanese (far enough away for complacency) nuclear power plant (dangerous enough for a frisson) had failed and, later, that a 104-year-old woman in Sweden had been offered a free place at nursery school.

The human analogue of the virus, which goes about its work automatically, is the hacker. The hacker's pleasure is to find his (or her?) way into a system thought to be foolproof by its owners until they find a spurious message on the screen, confidential information in the press, or sums of money going missing – according to the benignity or otherwise of the hacker.

The computer hacker is a direct descendant of the Phone Phreak, a breed dedicated to exploring the telephone network and its capabilities. Early phreaks were, I suppose 'chainers'; in the 50s before the days of STD we used to collect local dialling codes from telephone boxes, and make long-distance calls by constructing chains of codes from one exchange to the next.

Tapping the receiver rest of the phone at the right speed simulated the make-and-break action of the dial, enabling the well-tempered practitioner to make free calls – at least, from a call box.

With the advent of tone dialling in the 60s came the opportunity for whistling into the mouthpiece of the phone to simulate the tones. The most notorious (American) phreak was known as Kaptain Krunch, so called from the make of breakfast cereal from which he obtained the plastic whistle that produced the right frequencies to phool the phone.

Modern computer-controlled telephone systems made such tricks much harder, though the hacker/phreak is never far behind. At least call-barring saves a lot of money and heartache for those foafs whose au pairs left their employ just before the telephone bill arrived revealing calls home to Dare Nunder totalling hundreds – or thousands – of pounds.

And then there was the au pair's revenge: dialling the speaking clock and leaving it ticking for a month or so while the family was away.

The latest fright is web hacking; accessing confidential information, and inserting spurious data on to the web. The fact is that there is an enormous intellectual thrill to be derived from finding one's way through an almost infinite network by logical probing. If it were not so, there would never have been a Station X – Bletchley Park – and the mysteries of, for example, the structure of DNA and the human (or any other) genome would remain unsolved.

Some things happen by accident. I sought Spice City, an Indian Restaurant in Ely, on the net, and landed in a porn site in California. Then I started to receive unsolicited e-porn and had to hack it out by the roots.

Only the other day, I received an e-mail thanking me for my order for monthly pornpix, which would be charged to my card; if, however, I didn't want them, I had to send all my details to whoever it was. It's the electronic equivalent of driving old Mrs Defenceless to the bank so that she can pay cash for having her roof botched.

A foaf had a vacation job working in a power station. When switching in an alternator, it has to be run up to speed and the phases synchronised. This is done by watching three lamps flashing (he said) and comparing them with the three of the new alternator. The foaf somehow ran his alternator back to front; one set of lamps was flashing red, blue, yellow, and the other red, yellow, blue. Undeterred, he waited until both the red lamps were on, and threw the switch. There was the most tremendous explosion, and the alternator sailed out through the roof of the power station. Luckily no one was hurt.

Things usually sail out through the roof. A foaf was working in a gunpowder factory, where they use heavy flywheels to crush the ingredients. If something goes wrong with the mixture, the flywheel 'sails out through the roof'.

Another story told by a friend, who had worked in an explosives factory, is that the operatives sit on one-legged stools to stop them from going to sleep, for the effect of slumping over the workbench would be catastrophic. The logic here seems akin to the road accident prevention scheme whereby every car is equipped with a sharp spike in the centre of the steering wheel to promote careful driving.

Perhaps the same effect is achieved less drastically by the display 'How's my driving? Call 0800 blah blah'.

A friend of mine who is interested in the restoration of old buildings heard of a factory chimney which had to be removed because it was unsafe. Fantastic – all those lovely bricks. He went to negotiate and was overjoyed to find that he could demolish the chimney in return for the materials contained in it. The deal was clinched and he went to look at the chimney. And he then found that bricks from which the chimney was built were, not unnaturally on reflection, tapered to allow for the curvature of the structure.

However, he was luckier than the foaf who set up as a demolition contractor, and also, as it happens, undertook to remove a chimney. He had a brilliant idea: he sealed the base, filled it with water to a depth of a few feet, and put in an explosive charge. When he set off the charge, the force was distributed equally in all directions, a ring of bricks was shot out, and the chimney settled, slightly shorter than it had been before.

The same story is told of an IRA attempt to blow up an electricity pylon: a charge was placed on each of the four legs and set off. The effect was to shorten the pylon without interrupting the electricity supply.

And this puts one in mind of the four massive hydraulic jacks on which the Eiffel Tower stands, protected thereby against the wind, earthquakes, and any other unbalancing forces Mother Nature can throw at it. There are foafs who have *actually seen* the underground control room, or talked to disaffected human controllers who have been replaced by (much more efficient) computers.

As for the Leaning Tower of Pisa, it mustn't be allowed to fall over, but to restore it to the verticality it has never had would be the ruin of the city.

A building worker was on the ground in charge of that end of a rope and pulley mechanism for transporting building materials up and down. He was holding the rope and at the top was a barrel, which a mate loaded with rubble. On the occasion of which I am speaking, it seems that the barrel was loaded such that it was heavier than the man on the ground and he, not having the presence of mind to let go of the rope and step out of the way, was pulled up into the air. On reaching the top he struck his head on the pulley, and at the same time the impact of the barrel on the ground caused it to split so that its contents fell out. The balance was now such that the stunned worker fell to the ground, dragging the barrel up to the top again. When he reached the ground, he let go of the rope, and down came the barrel striking him a final blow.

The late Gerard Hoffnung told that story at the Oxford Union in 1958 but I first read it in bold type on the front page of the *Cambridge Daily News*, as the newspaper was called when I read the story in 1951. I remember this particularly, as I was acting as a guinea pig for some lip-reading classes at the time, and told the story with illustrations on the blackboard.

It purported to come from Aahrus, which is suspicious for, as I have said, in Denmark Aahrus jokes are as Irish jokes in England. At one time, the Hoffnung record was so well known that no one would have dared to tell the story as true, but it will doubtless be back any silly season now . . . and, in fact, Jan Brunvand tells me he's researching it in all its guises even as I write.

What goes up must come down, and there is a plethora of stories of things falling from the sky. Generally, they are live creatures, for that increases the wonder of the occurrence. The Fortean Society is dedicated to recording and retailing these happenings. For example:

> In Ancient Greece (200 AD), it rained fish for three days.
> In Bergen, Norway (1578), there was a shower of yellow mice.
> In Memphis, Tennessee (1877), thousands of snakes fell from the skies.
> In Maryland (1969), hundreds of dead ducks dropped on to the streets.
> In London (1977), it hailed tiny frogs. 'The brim of my husband's hat was full of them,' commented one lady.

From time to time, Our Science Correspondent explains that 'the animals were probably taken up in a water spout', which may be fine for raising fish, but is more puzzling for such specific faunal selections as yellow mice.

However, there is another category of falling things; the one-offs used to fill spaces in newspapers when they run out of garden sheds blazing.

> Johannesburg: A woman was gravely injured by a miniature pomeranian called Blackie. He had been hurled from the 14th floor of a block of flats. Residents reported that ice cubes and a guitar had also been deposited on passers by. (And . . . ?)

> Prague: Mrs Czermak was so distraught over her husband's unfaithfulness that she cast herself out of a third-storey window. Her suicide bid was unsuccessful; she is still alive and well, having landed on the errant Mr Czermak – who perished.

> Leningrad: A man was walking along a street, when he noticed something hurtling downwards from a high block of flats. Summing up the situation in a split second, he rushed forward and caught the descending object. Just as he had thought; it was a baby. And this was the second time he had caught one.

New York: A ham sandwich dropped from the Empire State Building cracked the slabs of the sidewalk.

London: A coin dropped from St Paul's sliced through workman's helmet.

Warsaw: A shopper was taken to hospital after a chicken fell from the window of a six-storey apartment and hit him on the head. After he had recovered from concussion, a nurse asked him what his job was. 'I'm a poultry breeder', he said.

Gravity has much to answer for. A foaf paid a five-figure sum for a bottle of wine at auction, and set it up in a glass case, tastefully lit. Unfortunately, the heat was too much for the cork, which dried out and fell in.

In the small town of Yellville, deep in the heart of the Ozark mountains of Arkansas, the foremost sporting and social event is the annual Turkey Drop. Each year a small low-flying aircraft circles above the town square, and watched by the eager crowd, releases 17 turkeys. The idea is that the turkeys fly down to be sportingly chased and caught by townspeople in time for Thanksgiving. However, the turkeys are neither good flyers nor quick thinkers and to the eternal grief of the Arkansas Humane Society most of them suffer fatal injuries.

There was one instance when a startled turkey soiled the man responsible for pushing them out, and angered him so much that he wrung its neck before throwing it out. Back in the 1950s, the AHS won the day and instead of dropping live turkeys, frozen ones were launched, each with a tiny parachute attached. Yet again, this was unsuccessful. The frozen birds fell so heavily that they became a danger to the crowd below; one smashed through a porch roof, another severely dented a car. But the worst experience of all was when the Chamber of Commerce responsible for the turkeys accidentally bought a flock whose wings had been clipped. This time there were no injuries: just universal death. One would really have thought that they could have got it right, especially with the AHS on their backs.

A couple had two geese, which they were fattening up for Christmas. But when the time came to dispatch them they realised that they couldn't bring themselves to do it. Instead they decided to give the geese an overdose of sleeping pills to kill them. They had a few gins to give them courage, waiting for the drugs to take effect, then returned to the geese and plucked them. Next morning, they were alarmed to find two nude geese dazedly wandering around the kitchen.

A man bought an electric blanket with dual controls enabling each sleeper to control the heat on his or her side of the bed. That night, he and his wife went to bed eager to try it out, but in the middle of the night the chap woke up sweating and exclaimed: 'What's wrong with this damned blanket? I keep turning it down and I'm getting hotter and hotter.' His amazed wife then revealed that she had been turning her own controls full on but was freezing to death.

Naturally, they were more than disappointed so the man vowed to take it back to the shop. The shopkeeper tested the blanket; it appeared to be working perfectly well; he could not understand the predicament. Determined not to be proved wrong, the man threw the blanket over the counter and demonstrated that the controls were not functioning properly. Then the shopkeeper saw the problem immediately: they'd put the blanket on upside down.

A hospital in Edinburgh used its ECT machine for over two years, reporting effects beneficial to the patients, before discovering that there was something wrong with the power supply and the machine had never worked.

There are many secret substances whose existence is known only to the favoured few, who let slip their knowledge as proof that they are privy to arcane secrets of their trade. The secret substance is a catalyst whose non-existence turns figments of the imagination into spurious knowledge.

Chemistry lecturers tell their wide-eyed classes of the perfect poison – it is tasteless, odourless, kills instantaneously, and immediately decomposes inside the body to everyday and therefore undetectable substances. If I remember rightly, it was trichloracetic acid.

All doctors know of the abortifacient drug, but keep it a deadly secret. And there is the secret substance which one can drop into an alcoholic drink without it impairing it in any way, save that it renders the presence of alcohol in the bloodstream undetectable by breath-alyser or other tests.

A public utility arranged for its customers to return their remittances in the same envelopes as they'd received their bills. Unfortunately, they all bounced back to their senders, because the coding dots applied by the Post Office for the initial delivery continued to control the sorting. It cost far more than it was supposed to save to disentangle that one.

A Mr Mahmud Razik Rashed, of Bethlehem, bought some flour in a local shop with which his wife baked bread for dinner. An hour or so later members of the family were violently sick, and a 12-year-old daughter who touched the bread fainted. When she came round she said that she had felt a strong electrical current coming from the loaf. The whole family rushed to the hospital for tests and then the police were called in. Their electrical expert applied a 220-volt tester to the flour – and the bulb lit up. I'm sure we could all do with some more information about that.

A young man successfully broke into a factory in New Addington, Surrey to steal cheese. The getaway was planned; he and his brother had two prams outside. Unfortunately, the two forgot one thing. It was snowing at the time and police simply followed the pram tracks.

Other criminals manage to operate just as unsuccessfully without having to work half as hard.

A would-be thief ran up to a senior citizen in Denver, Colorado, USA, forced open her mouth, removed her false teeth, and examined them. 'There ain't no gold here,' he complained, and handed them back to her.

Perhaps Colorado breeds gold-hunters of a particularly inventive nature, for it was there in 1874 that such a man stood trial – for cannibalism. And the judge lamented: 'There were only six democrats in the county and you ate five of them.'

The Falklands adventure, crisis or war, according to how you look at it, gave rise to a number of stories which have become muddled together so that one isn't sure whether they actually happened or not.

I am fairly certain I read of a pilot who was forced to use his ejection seat and, as a result of the impact, one of the physiological effects was that his eyesight was temporarily out of focus. He was convinced as he lay on the ground gathering himself together, that the sheep wandering about were actually Argentinians.

Another story concerns a group of marines who, hearing voices speaking in Spanish, went to ground, and stayed there for some time until they discovered that the voices were actually those of sheep. This may be some comment on what the marines thought of Argentinians, although it is a joke against themselves when it comes down to it.

Paul Smith told a story which he averred that he'd made up, through constant half-listening to the radio whilst doing something else over a period of weeks. He stated that the SAS had been moving around the islands without let or hindrance by the simple expedient of dressing up as sheep. When they found this out, the Argentinians began to shoot all the sheep they could find.

One evening, some students took the magnet out of a magnetron – a device containing a very powerful magnet and used to create short waves – and by presenting it to the window of an ironmonger's shop, were able to rearrange the display completely.

There is always someone who knew someone who met his death by pissing on to an electric railway, or cables of some sort. 'It got him', they used to say.

The following was related by a local barber, after a period of high winds across the fens:

>Farmer (to Old Fred, a farm worker): Well Fred, we gittin
>   plenty o'wind lately.
>
>Fred: What do you expect, bor? There ent any windmills
>   about now to use the blarsted stuff up.

A converse story is told in Haddenham (Cambridgeshire). The Great Mill and Nevill's Mill stood on opposite sides of the Aldreth Road. But Nevill's Mill had to be dismantled ' 'cos there weren't enough wind for the both on 'em'. The Great Mill is still turning.

A vicar, faced with a problem in complexity, decided that he should use the technology of the day, and called on the local computer centre. The problem was that his grave diggers were reporting that they could not find space for fresh graves in his graveyard, though church records and back-of-envelope calculations indicated that there should be more than enough room.

The local computer centre was much taken with this request and talent was brought to bear and a program written. Data was punched up including the dimensions of the standard coffin, and the program was run. Much to everyone's astonishment, the system reported that the cemetery was less than one third full.

The program was checked, and rechecked. It took a great deal of work to establish that the system was assuming that coffins were buried in the most economical way – vertically.

In America, an entire university class flopped in their maths exam because their calculators' batteries failed and began to claim that 2+2=5 (please explain). I take it that this story spread via those who were incensed that calculators were allowed in exams.

A Dutch veterinary surgeon was fined £140 for accidentally burning down a farm with a jet of flame from the rear end of a cow. He lit a match to test the gas coming out of a tube inserted in the cow, which was suffering from a badly swollen stomach. The flame set light to bales of hay in a barn and then burned down the whole farm, causing damage estimated at £45,000. The cow escaped with shock.

You will have observed the 'only-moments-before' syndrome. Whenever a lorry, tree, aeroplane or whatever crashes into a house it usually destroys a sofa or bed where 'only moments before' the relieved and thankful occupant had been resting or sleeping.

Unfortunately, people do get killed in such incidents, but if you monitor the newspaper reports you will find that small-scale local disasters are much more benign in that nine times out of ten they contain an 'only moments before'. And when an aeroplane, or coach, turns into an immolation horror, there are always plenty of people who were prevented from going on the trip because of a premonition, or a car that wouldn't start, or some other divine intervention.

In the few days after the Ufton Nervet rail disaster of 6 November 2004, several newspaper reports of lesser accidents were somewhat spuriously linked to it. A report on 12 November describes a train having to ' "screech to a halt" just four days *before* the Reading rail disaster' (italic mine). Another incident occurred at Exeter 'only six days after the Berkshire train crash' and 'on the same Paddington to

Penzance line as where the crash happened.' And another train "Screeched to a halt" ten days after. Since then, things seem to have gone quiet.

The effects of blast are peculiar and it was not unusual during the war to see walls that were standing with delicate objects balanced on protrusions. We have a set of glass grapefruit bowls which, the story goes, were reserved by the purchaser (who later gave them to my wife) the day before the shop was bombed. The following day, they went round to the shop to collect the bowls, only to find it a heap of rubble – but, what is this? The sturdy mahogany counter has survived the attack and – you've guessed it – there underneath are the undamaged fruit bowls.

This whole story reveals a truth about our reasoning. Wonderful as it may be that the bowls weren't damaged, we seem to forget first, all the things that *were* damaged and, second, that if the bowls hadn't survived nobody would have been surprised. It's the difference between the personal and statistical ways of looking at things. So-and-so may be surprised and delighted that he's been cast as Jesus in the Passion Play, but *somebody* had to take that (and others every other) part.

'What on earth are you doing here?'
'Everybody's got to be somewhere.'

Just as the famous Orson Welles *War of the Worlds* broadcast spread panic in America before the Second World War so, it appears, were people taken in by the *Alternative 3* programme shown on ITV in June 1977 (it was originally scheduled for 1 April). Personally, I found it hard to be fooled by the hammy interviews, but the principle will serve to reinforce the story that human artefacts were found on the moon by both Americans and Russians – and that both are keeping quiet about it. Could the story have started in the [somewhat silly] 1960 film *The First Man on the Moon*, where Kenneth More landed – and found an empty baked beans tin?

The reciprocal of the artefacts-on-the-moon story is the belief that the whole of the moon landing programme was simulated in television studios. This is quite widespread – especially, I'm told, in Mexico, where they laugh at you if you suggest that it really happened. The purpose of the elaborate fabrication is not stated.

No book of ULs would be complete without some reference to 'parascience'. An excellent feature in *New Scientist* summed up the 'evidence' for the Bermuda Triangle, Flying Saucers and Spoon-bending, not to mention the Miracle of Fatima. But these are isolated subjects in parascience, which covers a vast range of unexplained happenings and artefacts.

Its literature grows as rapidly as that of any of the more conventional sciences. Disproving such a widely-reported phenomenon as flying saucers is difficult; proving it, if the evidence should become available, would be much easier.

You can demonstrate ways of making crop circles, but that doesn't prove that they were made that way. People love to believe the unbelievable – six things before breakfast, even – the Loch Ness Monster (just one of it, and of incredible age); the Beast of Bramerton with its cloven hooves and unstoppable progress; pumas and panthers (literally big cats).

Stonehenge as an eclipse-predictor is either a colossal coincidence, or an example of how proper analysis can enable a topic to pass from parascience to science (though discovery of its possible mathematical purpose by no means answers all the questions about Stonehenge).

What is really interesting about Stonehenge (and other 'primitive' structures) is that the people who built it had enough of an overview of what they wanted to achieve (in terms of celestial orientation, for example) to be able to design it, and a means of recording relevant events which could be handed down from one generation to the next where a cycle of some events is longer than an individual's life-span. Or was it built first and then 'explained' in terms of any old phenomenon that happened to fit? I think not.

It is commonly felt that conventional religion has let us down in not providing the answers to the basic questions mankind dares to ask it. Religious faith, it seems, is not enough; parascientific faith comes much more easily, to some. According to John Morley, 'The next great task of science is to create a religion for mankind'.

But remember, faith and proof are two sides of the same coin, not the bases of two opposing ways of looking at things.

Christianity – and perhaps other systems of belief for all I know – seems to be going the wrong way, if church attendance is any indication. Here's a view. When the church was strong it was because the priests were men of learning, and the people were oppressed, believing in hellfire and damnation. That's not a good thing in itself – what *was* good was that people were grabbed by the *mystery* of it.

Today, it is clear that among the few the Christian message is just as strong, but what about the many? Can it be that there is little to attract them to the church because it is too like real life? What the church ought to be doing is developing its mystery, not trying to reach the people with happy-clappyness and tales of world famine and pestilence – that's like staying at home and watching the news.

The mystery embodied, for example, in such things as the architecture, stained glass, tombs and memorials, religious works of art, ethereal music, sheer antiquity, the odour of sanctity, and the words of the King James Bible is what makes churchgoing a spiritual experience – and gives us some idea of what our forebears must have felt. There is still likely to be some majesty in the architectural environment, but what goes on within it may have the effect of degrading that majesty. Restore the beauty and the mysticism, and it may well be that therefrom springs the atmosphere wherein one can once again believe six impossible things before breakfast. If anyone wants to be happy-clappy and third-world outreach, let this be achieved outside the mystical environment. It's the spiritual analogue of fox hunting.

As I've said before, serendipity has always played an important part in my research, and shortly after composing the above analysis, I came across a letter in the *Sunday Telegraph* from Revd Peter Mullen, Chaplain to the Stock Exchange, who kindly allows me to quote:

Tediously twanging guitars; doggerel choruses on overhead projectors; the sub-liturgical slow handclap; modern prayers that drag along like a lump of dead meat; the vicar's banana split smile as he [or she] invites us all to kiss and cuddle; patronising sermons sometimes delivered with the aid of a glove puppet; the altar put in the nave, so destroying the concept of sacred space . . . Yes, there is a hell. It's just like church.

7

Really Motoring

> The modern motor car is in all cases a comfortable
> conveyance, and in the more expensive types it embodies
> a greater degree of luxury than any other medium of
> locomotion, except perhaps the Atlantic liner.
>
> Edward Cressy – *Discoveries and*
> *Inventions of the Twentieth Century**

Has any single invention had such a profound effect on mankind as the motorcar? (Well, the internal combustion engine, perhaps.) Apart from its superficial value for getting things from A to B, it has its role as a symbol for sex, status and Lord knows what-all. I look forward to the role of the motor car in shaping society coming into perspective; we will no doubt learn something exceedingly profound about ourselves when it does.

As befits its stature, the motorcar and the way of life it has engendered have provided several widespread ULs, many of which have already enjoyed a rich and varied life.

A foaf saw a motor car advertised in the local press for £5. Of course, he couldn't believe his eyes – this year's model? All those extras? Well, if it was true, he was on to a good thing; somebody had to be there first and it could be him. So he rushed round to the address, and there was this woman, and she showed him the car, and the registration documents and so on, and it all seemed to be in order. Without asking too many questions, he gave her the fiver, and she gave him a receipt, and he drove it away. Later, he found out the truth – the woman's husband had left her, and asked her to sell his car and send him the proceeds.

In another version of the £5 car, the truth is made only too plain before the purchase. 'The car's down in the garage,' the woman says. 'But there's one thing I must tell you before you look at it – my poor (choke) dear husband (choke) committed suicide in it . . . '

And it needs cleaning out somewhat.

* The first edition of which, somewhat ambitiously, appeared in 1914.

One evening Alec Popple came to me in great excitement: 'Did you see that advertisement in the paper for a Volkswagen for £10? There must be some mistake.' We looked at it together, and couldn't see what the catch was, so we went off to view the car, found it, tried it, asked: 'Why is it only £10?' 'It's a misprint' she said, shattering our dreams.

An emancipated Edwardian motoring UL. The Vicar of D— was cycling along one evening, when he came across a stranded motorist whose acetylene lamps had run out of water. Having ascertained the nature of the problem, 'That's easy,' he said, 'we can use the water with which the Good Lord provided us.' Making sure that the coast was clear, he stood on tiptoes on the running-board, and peed into the container. 'That's all I've got,' he said. 'You'd better do the other side.' The motorist removed her goggles. 'I'm awfully sorry,' she said, 'the Good Lord forgot to make the proper provision.' A member of the suffragette set, no doubt.

A foaf had a vintage Austin – mechanically immaculate, but body-work tatty. Well, he was driving along – outskirts of Nottingham actually – when he was stopped by the police. They had a good look at his car: tyres OK, steering good, lights working, nothing falling off – couldn't find anything wrong. 'Right,' they said. 'We want to test

your speedometer and brakes. Drive along at a steady thirty and we'll follow you. Then when we blow the horn, you do an emergency stop.' So the foaf did as he was bid and, hearing an almighty horn blast stepped on the anchors. There was a most tremendous crash as the Police car ran into the back of his Austin. It was, of course, another vehicle which had blown its horn.

Life imitates art again; I heard that tale in the fifties, and in the late seventies, when I was a magistrate, I sat on a case wherein the man whose car had been run into by the testing police car was giving evidence for the prosecution of the allegedly careless police driver.

A young foaf went for a driving test with his motorcycle. 'Drive round the block,' said the tester, 'and when you see me step out into the road, do your emergency stop.' So the motorcyclist rode round the block, but on returning to the appointed place was surprised to see a crowd gathering in that normally quiet street. By the roadside was a mixture of bodies and a motorcycle. The tester had stepped out in front of the wrong rider.

The normal practice in this country when one is selling a car with a noisy gearbox (so I'm told) is to fill it with sawdust. But a friend of mine tells me that he has heard, once from a Chilean and once from a Venezuelan, that the South American custom is to fill the gearbox with mince. There's opulence for you.

In the days of my youth, a group of us used to hunt for interesting cars in the quiet lanes of East Anglia in my 1923 Rover 8. We would often hear of elusive cars which had been bought new before the war (*ie* pre-1914) and kept immaculately by their proud owners. At the beginning of the war (*ie* 1939) they had been laid up – raised on blocks, covered in grease and dust sheets. But the old man (if it was an old woman, she had had a chauffeur) had died, and it was found that he had left instructions in his will that the precious car should be burnt on a ceremonial pyre after his funeral. We never tracked the tale to its source.

A foaf was getting ready to go out one evening, when he noticed from his bedroom window that there was a car blocking his drive. As he had some time to spare, he ignored it, expecting it to go away. However he found that it was still there an hour later, and as he could see no signs of life, he down to investigate. There, inside, was a couple, coupled. 'Thank God you've come,' gasped the man. 'Something's gone in my back, and I can't move.' So the foaf went back and called the police, and they called an ambulance, and the fire brigade. The upshot of it was that the firemen had to cut the top off the car to lift the man out. While they were waiting for the other stretcher, the officer-in-charge said to the woman: 'I'm frightfully sorry that we've had to cut up your husband's car.' She smiled wanly, and replied: 'That's all right. It's not my husband.'

The Automobile Association regularly receives requests from people wanting unusual routes to their destinations, but none quite so bizarre as that from the woman who wanted to travel from Birmingham to Bristol – a distance of some 80 miles – without having to turn right. But, being trained to help all drivers at all times, the AA staff was able to oblige, making the woman's journey 100 miles longer.

This same obsessive fear of turning right is attributed to J Edgar Hoover, who, it is said, employed a complete entourage of route-planners to assist him on his journeys. Would you entrust your FBI to a man like that?

Another of the many J Edgar Hoover stories suggests that when a television set was first installed in his office, he was always calling in the engineers because it refused to come on immediately he turned the switch. They soon fitted a switch which gave instant control of sound and image, the set being left on all the time. Bloke's a menace.

As befits the king of cars, the Rolls-Royce has a number of stories all of its own. Henry Royce used to go down to the works just before knocking-off time on Saturday, cast an eye over the stock of chassis frames and say: 'Well, boys, which one am I going home on today?' And before they left the works, they had built him a car to use that weekend.

The Rolls of legend has a sealed bonnet, which must never be opened except at the factory. And if any driver not trained by the works should take the wheel, the guarantee is instantly void.

Not, of course, that there needs to be a guarantee. There is a well-known Rolls-Royce on tour in Spain when a half-shaft (sometimes the crankshaft) broke, just outside Madrid. So the family secured accommodation for the night, and sent a telegram to Derby. At daybreak, two immaculately-dressed mechanics flew in with tools and spares, and the family tour was able to continue with hardly a hitch. When asked for the bill, there came the reply: 'No charge, sir. Rolls-Royce half-shafts (crankshafts) *never* break.' The fact is that there were plenty of Rolls-Royce breakdowns; the cars were not as trouble-free as the man in the street believed, but the company strove to make the reality match the image.

Now I'll tell you a true one, and I do know to whom it happened (in the seventies). His Rolls-Royce broke down on the M1 near Newport Pagnell. He telephoned Derby. 'I should go to a garage, if I were you,' they said. 'Hey, wait a minute,' he remonstrated. 'What about the half-shaft that broke in Spain?' 'Oh yes,' they replied, 'we can send a mechanic if you want, but it'll cost you £100 a day. I should go to a garage if I were you.'

A foaf was going through the customs when he noticed a disturbance – there was this immaculate man, and his befurred wife, and his Rolls-Royce, and the customs-men were going through it with the proverbial fine toothcomb. And what a fuss the owner was making. And as the foaf watched, he saw the customs officials discover the specially strengthened springs, and so examining the mudguards and body panels, and finding that underneath they were made of nothing less than sheets of gold. The smugglers had been detected.

A foaf was motoring along, when the stream of traffic slowed to a halt, apparently because of some altercation between the driver of a Rolls-Royce and another motorist. One alighted, and twisted off the other's wing-mirror. The other, not to be outdone, did the same to his opponent. As if in slow motion, each perpetrated some unpleasantness on the other's vehicle; the other retaliated. Never a word was spoken. A crowd gathered in silence. At last, when all the accessories on each car had been smashed, the motorists shook hands, got into their respective vehicles and, with the ovation of the crowd ringing in their ears, drove away.

A large chauffeur-driven car pulls up in the forecourt of Farnham railway station, Surrey, and the chauffeur opens the door for his immaculately-dressed City boss. They stride over to the platform and when the train arrives, the gent boards and removes the wellington boots he has worn while travelling from his estate. The chauffeur takes them and goes back to the car. The gent settles down in his compartment, nods to fellow passengers, opens his briefcase – and finds that he has forgotten to pack his shoes. He was last seen at Waterloo Station shuffling through the ticket barrier with the remains of his Financial Times wrapped round his feet.

Another City gent had a large estate uphill from Reading Station.

Every morning, he would kid himself that he was getting exercise by cycling to the station – downhill all the way. And every evening one of the estate workers would be waiting for him at the station with the bicycle in the back of the Land Rover.

In the first version I heard of such a story, the man had five bicycles which were collected once a week. But how he got home each evening was not reported.

A man staggered out of a pub in Knaresborough. From nowhere, a policeman materialised and uttered those dreaded words: 'Would you mind blowing into this, Sir?' Summoning up as much dignity as possible, the man blearily blew. 'Thank you sir, it needed warming up,' said the playful policeman. It was his glove. The man got the message, and didn't attempt to drive.

The owner of a stately home (not open to the public) is somewhat annoyed to see a car and caravan turn into his drive, park on the verge, and disgorge a full load of family, which proceeds to unpack the well-known folding chairs, tables, gas stoves *etc* and prepare a meal.

However, he does nothing, but takes the number of the vehicle, and then traces the owner via the police. In the fullness of time, he loads his car with equipment and family, sets off for the suburban semi wherein his unwelcome visitors live, and holds a picnic in their drive.

Lord Montagu tells a similar story about the owner of a stately home which was open to the public. He was incensed by the mess and litter left by a party of visitors. He made a note of their number, found their address, and the following week he and his family went there and held a noisy and messy picnic on the front lawn of their suburban house. Later, I heard of a local farmer who was said to have done the same thing.

Talking of trippers, a party of Cambridge people on a gasworks outing to Yarmouth had to help one of their number back to the coach because he was helplessly drunk. On reaching Cambridge, they took him home and put him to bed to sleep it off. When he woke, he was astonished to find himself at home in Cambridge because he hadn't been a member of the coach party but was in the middle of a fortnight's holiday in Yarmouth and had merely fallen in with the crowd of his workmates who happened to be on the works outing. Meanwhile, his wife had reported him missing to the police.

There is a reciprocal version of this tale. A couple went on holiday and thought it would be rather fun to spend a day on an advertised mystery coach trip. So they bought tickets and set off in high hopes – only to find that the mystery destination was their home town. So rather than paying exorbitant rates for the local food, they decided to pop home and cook themselves a meal there. And somehow, they managed to miss the coach back.

There is nothing so fearsome as being the last on a waiting coach. As life imitates art, my wife and I went on an educational visit with a local organisation, and ended up with an hour or so to spare in a village unknown to all on the coach except us – we had relations there. 'You can all go and explore,' said the organiser, 'but be back at 4.30 sharp.' So we went off for a cup of tea and exchange of family news, arriving back at the appointed 4.30 sharp to rows of the stony faces of those who had found the stop, shall we say, 'unexciting'.

A foaf was touring with a caravan on the continent, and ran short of time to catch the ferry back to England, so he had to drive furiously through the night, with his wife having a kip in the caravan.

At length, he had to stop for a pee, and while he was out, his wife woke up and also felt the call of nature. So she left the fastness of the caravan and went into the bushes. And her husband returned and drove off into the night. Luckily (in some ways) the next car along was a police-car but she still had some difficulty in explaining what had happened.

In a reciprocal version of this story, it is the tired man who is resting in the caravan, and the wife who is driving. For some reason or other, she is forced to stop suddenly, and her husband very unwisely emerges in his underpants to see what the trouble is. As if on a signal, she chooses that moment to drive away.

Back home again, we exchange foreign, gun-slinging policemen for the ever-reliable RAC.

An embarrassed motorist ran into the RAC office at Southwaite, Cumbria to tell the superintendent that he had lost his wife. They had been travelling along the M6 from Manchester to Glasgow when the man had decided to stop at a service station to use the lavatory. He quickly returned, jumped back in the car and drove off. Some forty miles later he had missed his wife. The RAC phoned the service station but she wasn't there, so they set off to find her. They had just started out when the man glimpsed his wife in a car travelling in the opposite direction. When they eventually caught up with her she said that she had decided to get out too, but when she returned, the car was gone.

A woman, having to journey to Manchester, was obliged to stay the night at an hotel. So she booked in and was told that, as the builders were in, many rooms were unavailable, and that she had been allocated the bridal suite. This imposing room was furnished with an Adam fireplace, velvet armchairs and gold-plated taps in the bathroom but it lacked a wardrobe – presumably the frenzied guests usually hurled their clothes into corners. The woman phoned room service to ask for some coat hangers and some hooks to hang them on. 'Yes madam, I'll have some hangers brought to you right away,' said room service. 'But hangers are no use without a rail,' said the woman, 'what am I to hang the hangers on?' There was a pause, and then room service replied brightly: 'Guests usually use the chandelier'.

Hotels and the like above a certain standard really understand the meaning of service. John Mortimer once invited me to lunch at Simpson's in the Strand. My way was politely barred by the head waiter: 'I'm sorry sir, you can't go into the dining-room without a jacket.' With the presence of mind usually reserved for hindsight, I commanded: 'Then please fetch me one' There was a short pause, and a waiter's jacket was silently brought and held up for me – it was almost large enough, but the tightness under the arms was far outweighed by the triumph.

A foaf and his girlfriend were on holiday in a little village in Cornwall. One morning, they planned to drive to the large town nearby to do some shopping; however, they found that the car wouldn't start, so the girlfriend went to the village shop to buy the necessary groceries while the foaf started work on the car. When she returned, she saw legs sticking out from under the car, so she administered a playful squeeze to their confluence, and went into the cottage, where she was astounded to see the foaf enjoying a cup of coffee. He explained that the man under the car was a kindly neighbour, and that he should be coming in any minute now to have his coffee and discuss the car problem with the foaf. The girlfriend explained what had happened, and they sat and waited for the man to come indoors, wondering how to explain the attack. But he didn't come, and he didn't come, so they went out to investigate and found that he was still under the car. They were unable to attract his attention, so they dragged him out, whereupon he came round, nursing a large bruise on his head. 'Something made me bump my head on the sump' he mumbled confusedly. 'Come indoors and have a drink,' they replied, exchanging glances.

A Surrey couple had their car stolen from their front drive. Four days later it reappeared – with two theatre tickets on the front seat and a note which read: 'Sorry. We had to take your car in an emergency. Please accept the tickets with our apologies.' A few days later they used the tickets and returned to find their home stripped, even to the curtains.

That story appeared in the late 70s, and circulated widely. I heard it several times, and it was reported in the press, but without any details of who, when or where – all the marks of a UL.

An elderly lady who usually came into Cambridge to shop by bus decided that, as it was such a beautiful day, she would travel on her unaccustomed bicycle. She parked it in St Mary's Passage and went off to do her shopping. Because she was not used to this mode of transport, she forgot her bicycle and went home by bus; it was only when she had had lunch that she remembered that she had left her bicycle outside Great St Mary's Church. So she took the bus back in the afternoon to collect the bicycle and was very relieved to see that it was still there, especially, she noticed, as she had forgotten to lock it. She went into the church to thank God that her bicycle was still outside, and when she came out, it had gone.

A woman, visiting her sister's family, had stayed much longer than intended, and was then faced with the long drive home in darkness. She hurriedly said her goodbyes, jumped into her car, and sped off homewards. Immediately she noticed another car right on her tail, obviously taking the same route, for it followed her out of town and on to the main road. Although she was going quite fast, he seemed to want to overtake, so she slowed down to let him pass. The car behind slowed down too. So she put her foot down thinking he'd stay back.

The car behind gathered speed – and stayed just behind her. She tried other tactics to try to shake off this joker, and was just about to stop when her annoyance turned to fear – what was this driver really up to? So she accelerated again, and drove flat out the rest of the way home – the pursuing headlights ever shining in her rear view mirror. By the time she reached home she was so frightened that she drove the car straight up on to the footpath, over the flower border, into the garden and up to the front door where she sat and blew on the horn until her bleary-eyed husband came outside. Just then the other driver got out. 'What's going on?' enquired the husband. 'This man his followed me all the way home. 40 miles!' his wife frantically replied. The driver spoke: 'I followed your wife because just as I was going in to my house I noticed somebody hiding in the back of her car.' He opened the door and there, crouching ashen-faced on the floor, was a very shady character indeed.

Sometimes, this character turns out to be a mad axeman, sometimes dressed in women's clothing for greater confusion.

One for the road. A foaf was touring on the continent, snaking along one of those mountain roads with a sheer drop on one side. Rather too suddenly, he came upon a sharp bend to the left and not altogether wisely took it on the inside. That day the gods were smiling for, coming from the other direction, was another car whose driver had been similarly surprised by the bend and had taken it on the *out*side. So they crossed on a blind corner, each on the wrong side of the road. Somewhat shaken, both stopped, got out, walked back to the bend, shook hands silently, turned and, without a word, walked back to their cars and drove on.

8

The Animal Kingdom

Animals are such agreeable friends – they ask
no questions, they pass no criticisms
GEORGE ELIOT

A great deal of energy has been expended on examining the truth of the story that Jonah was swallowed by a whale. Those who think they're in the know say that a whale's throat is too small to take a man. However, the sperm whale, or cachalot, does have a throat of sufficient size and it is said that the skeleton of an 18-foot shark was found in the stomach of one of these animals. (It is also said that a man in a suit of armour was found in a shark.)

In February 1891, one James Bartley fell off a whaler and could not be found. However, the crew at last caught a whale, and started to prepare it that night. The next day they attached tackle to the whale's stomach, and hoisted it on board. Suddenly, the sailors were startled by something in it which gave spasmodic signs of life. (Shades of the original whale-tumour story.) Of course – it was none other than James Bartley. However, he was unconscious, and when he revived had to be restrained as a raving lunatic, but after three weeks of kind and careful treatment he had entirely recovered from the shock and resumed his duties. But the whale's gastric juices had bleached his skin and he never recovered his natural appearance.

Frank T Bullen was more lucky, in a way. He was first mate of the good whaler *Cachalot*, and was with a crew in a small boat seeking to entrap one of the parent ship's live namesakes. The monster smashed the boat, and FTB became involved with the 'titanic convulsions of the dying cachalot'. He was much afraid of being swallowed whole, but wasn't. He was rescued and put to bed for [the customary period of] three weeks: 'In my sleep I would undergo the horrible anticipation of sliding down that awful, cavernous mouth over again, often waking with a shriek and drenched with sweat.' He returned to work looking ten years older. I wouldn't be surprised if his 'hair had turned white over night'.

But what of Jonah? It is the popularisers of the Bible who assumed that a 'great fish' is a whale. And the 'village atheists' have pounced on this and said that the whale has a small throat, therefore it could not have swallowed Jonah, therefore the whole Bible is untrue.

Make no mistake, Jonah was swallowed by a great *dahg* (fish) and not by a *taneem*, the word translated as 'whale' in Ezek 32: 2, or *taneen* Gen 1: 21 and Job 7: 12. (Both these words are elsewhere translated as 'dragon' or 'serpent'.) So Jonah's *dahg* could have been a cachalot.

But to further confuse those who would tell tales of men being swallowed by whales of one sort or another as an oblique affirmation of Old Testament faith, John Miles has suggested that in any case the Book of Jonah is a parody. For a start, instead of expressing his reluctance to be a prophet in anguished eloquence, Jonah remains silent. And the idea that he actually *pays* for his passage to Tarshish seems as ludicrous to Miles as if Moses had thrown water on the burning bush. And so we are taken from unlikely detail to unlikely detail until the Lord finally comforts Jonah with a gourd, only to send a worm to destroy it the following day, not to mention the wind and the sun.

If the Book of Jonah is a parody – and Miles puts forward a scholarly case for it being so – it is a very amusing one, taken in the context of the minor prophets of the Hebrew Bible.

Writing of the whale Revd J G Wood uses the following words:

> The jaw opens very far back, and in a large Whale is about sixteen feet in length, seven feet wide, and ten or twelve feet in height, affording space, as has been quaintly remarked, for a jolly-boat and her crew to float in.

And Ernest Protheroe writes:

> The length of the baleen (16 feet) gives some idea of the size of the Whale's mouth, and it is not without reason that sailors assert that a ship's jolly-boat with a crew complete could row into the cavernous aperture without touching the sides.

I wonder if the two jolly-boats are related?

While wallowing in the luxury of late-Victorian natural history writers – fine as long as you can stop when you want to – let us look at Wood, an entertainingly anecdotal writer, on the grey parrot:

> Its power of initiating all kinds of sounds is really astonishing. I have heard a parrot imitate, or rather reproduce, in rapid succession the most dissimilar of sounds, without the least effort and with the most astonishing truthfulness. He could whistle lazily like a street idler, cry prawns and shrimps as well as any costermonger, creak like an ungreased 'sheave' in the pulley that is set in the blocks through which ropes run for sundry nautical purposes, or keep up a quiet and gentle monologue about his own accomplishments with a simplicity of attitude that was most absurd. Even in the imitation of louder noises he was equally expert, and could sound the danger whistle or blow off steam with an astonishing accuracy. Until I came to understand the bird, I used to wonder why some invisible person was always turning an imperceptible capstan in my close vicinity, for the parrot had also learned to imitate the grinding of the capstan bars and the metallic clink of the catch as it falls rapidly upon the cogs. As for the ordinary accomplishments of parrots, he possessed them in perfection, but in my mind his most perfect performance was the imitation of a dog having his foot run over by a cartwheel. First there came the sudden, half-frightened bark, as the beast found itself in unexpected danger, and then the loud shriek of pain, followed by the series of howls that is popularly termed 'pen and ink'. Lastly the howls grew fainter as the dog was supposed to be limping away, and you really seemed to hear him turn the corner and retreat into the distance. The memory of the bird must have been most tenacious, and its powers of observation far beyond the common order; for he could not have been a witness to such a canine accident more than once.

Unless the parrot 'did' the cart, I don't see how the listener could have known what had happened to the dog. One of the most amazing things I've ever heard was the lyre bird, presented by David Attenborough, imitating forest clearance with a chain saw, and the sound of the camera shutter. How and why does it decide what to imitate? Does it have to practise? How does it get the noises in the correct sequence (understanding cause and effect)? How does it know how well it's doing? And what makes it perform the imitation anyway?

Just because animals can't talk human doesn't mean they lack intellect. In fact, one could argue that the need even *more* intellect to be able to find their way around and reason their decisions without language. I have seen a parrot that appeared to hold a 'proper' conversation, rather than repeating the same phrases at random – parrot fashion.

Another parrot story:

Horsedrawn tram services in Douglas, Isle of Man, were disrupted when the horses, which usually stopped only at the conductor's whistle, kept drawing up at a point between two halts. It was found that a parrot lived in a house overlooking the promenade and had got the signal whistle off to a tee.

A friend of mine nearly stepped out into the traffic when I whistled my imitation of a pelican crossing.

From parrots (and pelicans) to penguins. All the world loves a penguin, owing to the fact that it's bipedal and dresses for dinner. Those of us hedged around with property and possessions turn all shades of green with envy at someone who can swim a few thousand miles, pop out on to an island, and set up house – just like that.

The young son of a foaf arrived home from a visit to the Zoo, dumped his duffel-bag, and tucked into a plate of bangers and mash. While trying to elicit from him whether or not he had had a good day, and what he had seen, his mother noticed a movement in the duffel-bag which was lying in the corner of the room. On investigation, the bag was found to contain a baby penguin. The lad denied all knowledge of it – no, he hadn't picked it up when nobody was looking. So his mother telephoned the Zoo, and found that they still had their full complement of penguins . . .

This bears some resemblance to an incident which occurred a century or so ago, when a man strolling in Regent's Park came across a large snake curled up in a flower-bed. He called a keeper, who called other keepers, and they stood guard over the sleeping reptile while someone hot-footed it to the Zoo to fetch the snake keeper. And although the snake was captured and taken to the Zoo, it wasn't one of theirs. This story was reported in the press, and suddenly snake-finding became a epidemic. A London & North-Western railway guard found a 22 foot boa-constrictor in his van. And the son of an MP found a huge snake in one of the rooms of his father's London house.

The penguin story may have some affinity with the account of the man who was walking in St John's Wood, when he saw a penguin waddling along. The penguin approached him on his stroll. Soon they saw a policeman, and the man inquired what he should do with the penguin. 'Take him to the Zoo, if I were you, Sir,' said the policeman. So the man did. The next day, the policeman was surprised to see the man coming towards him with the penguin still walking by his side. 'I thought I said you should take the penguin to the Zoo,' said the policeman. 'I did,' replied the man, 'and this afternoon, we're going to the pictures.'

Compare this with the shaggy dog story of the barman who – after much preamble – was given a lobster by a grateful customer:

> 'Thank you very much, sir, I'll take it home for supper.'
> 'Oh no, don't do that, barman – er, I mean, I'd rather you didn't. You see, he's had his supper. Just put him to bed.'

Dogs are sacred in our culture and nothing about them is more sacred than their ability to foretell the future, to warn of impending calamities, and to sense 'instinctively' the death of a master or mistress who may chance at that moment to be far away. And, of course, there is their ability to find their way borne over immense distances:

> In 1923 a collie named Bobbie, lost by his owners while they were on holiday in Wolcott, Indiana, USA, turned up at the family home in Silverton, Oregon six months later, after covering a distance of some 2,000 miles (3,200 km). The dog, later identified by householders who had looked after him along the route, apparently travelled back through the states of Illinois, Iowa, Nebraska and Colorado, before crossing the Rocky Mountains in the depths of winter and then continuing through Wyoming and Idaho.

'Apparently' is a cautionary word. It means 'I don't have any evidence for this, but I'd like you to believe it for the sake of the story, though I'm a bit doubtful myself'. But Bobbie seems to be better documented than Hector, although Hector's feat is that much more amazing:

> How do pet dogs and cats find their way home over immense distances? The record is held by a terrier called Hector. He hitched a ride in a ship from Vancouver, Canada, to Yokohama, Japan, to be reunited with his owner . . .

No answer is given to the original question. If we allow that there is some homing mechanism enabling dogs to find their way over dry land – after all, the birds and the bees are proven navigators – it is hard to see how a dog would know the destination of a ship.

I followed a blind man and his guide dog down the steps to the Eastbound platform at Great Portland Street underground station, curious to know how the dog would choose the right train. Imagine my delight when I noticed that the indicator board showed that the first train was to Barking.

Homing cats, too, are oft reported, returning, for some reason or other, to the house where they lived before the family moved. This is in stark contrast to the lost and found columns of the newspapers and newsagents' windows, which testify to the fact that many cats can't find their way home from the next street.

It is, however, possible to grow rich by catching cats and selling them to 'the vivisectionist' (is that a trade in its own right?) and if anyone tells of such an occurrence the catnapper will as like as not glide away in a Rolls-Royce. Apparently, it gives comfort to the tearful late owner of the abducted pet to know that it has departed in the service of mankind's thirst for knowledge, and in a style to which its late owner can never aspire.

A woman living in a bed-sit was rather concerned as to how she should dispose of her recently deceased cat. So when a friend suggested that they bury it in his garden she took up the offer straight away. She carefully laid the corpse in a shoe box, placed it in a carrier bag, and set off for the bus station. When she discovered that she'd just missed her bus, she popped into the large store on the High Street to find a little something for her friend. She found it, took it to the desk, paid, and was about to leave when she missed her bag. Within moments, the assistant had alerted the store detective while a growing throng of staff and onlookers began to search the floor. When the store detective arrived she seized her chance: 'Quick! Up to the Ladies,' she said, 'we'll catch her this time.' And so they did. The cleaning lady unlocked the cubicle door, and there was the would-be thief, unconscious, with the bag at her feet and the dead cat in her lap.

Coolidge's cat was of an unspecified colour:

> After being elected President of the United States (1923), Calvin Coolidge invited several unsophisticated friends to dine at the White House. Having seen him pour tea into his saucer, the guests did likewise. The President added cream and sugar, and so did they. Then he put his saucer on the floor – which was when they realised that his pet cat was sitting under the table.

This story has turned up more than once; it has to be told about some well-known figure, and reflects either upon the charming simplicity or the crawling sycophancy of the great man's followers. Sometimes the Great Man himself is charmingly simple and, finding a finger-bowl before him on the table at a banquet, drinks its contents. Whereupon everyone else follows suit. The custom of leaving the bottom button of the waistcoat undone started, they tell me, with Edward VII's inability to fasten his, owing to embonpoint. It's the reciprocal of the Emperor's new clothes.

As for drinking out of saucers, more than one story is told of the cat artist Louis Wain attending a tea-party where he was offered milk in a saucer for a joke. Mr Wain was Not Amused.

A lady washed her poodle regularly and to dry him thoroughly, she used to place him in the gas oven with the door open for just a few minutes in order to 'fluff him up'. This worked well for some years, until the lady's son presented her with a microwave oven. She decided to try it out on the poodle, so after his bath she placed him inside the oven, closed the door, set the controls and turned it on. The poodle exploded.

This story spread like wildfire as the microwave oven became commonplace and, as like as not, the victim was a poodle. Sometimes it is stated that it cooks from the inside outwards which lends an aura of science to the tale.

As the world becomes nastier, there are periodical convictions of people who have put animals in microwave ovens . . . one shudders to think how many are never apprehended; one of the more unpleasant examples of life imitating art. Small animals go round in the washing machine as well, 'emerging bedraggled and groggy but none the worse for the experience'. It's not long since a five-year-old boy was reported as having a turn, though how he shut the door behind him and switched on the machine is not revealed. Perhaps it was that ubiquitous 'little sister'.

Back to poodles. A lady travelling on the subway had her little poodle with her. She was anxious not to seem too protective, and so was leading it rather than carrying it. However, while it was summoning up enough energy to leap from the platform to the carriage, the doors closed on its lead, and before anyone realised what was happening the train set off and the dog was dragged to its death.

An old Walter Gabriel with a poodle had buttenholed someone by an automatic level crossing, and absent-mindedly slipped the dog's leash over the end of the boom. The dog cowered as the 10.30 for York thundered through, and then yelped as the boom swung aloft with its live load. Walter and friend were leaping up and down but couldn't reach the unfortunate poodle. Off went Walter to the emergency telephone and explained the emergency. 'Don't worry,' said the voice at the other end, 'he'll be down again when the 10.53 comes along.'

The father of a friend of mine is an insurance broker – he's in fire, but has a colleague in the motor department who tells the following story.

They received a claim from a motorist the front of whose Mini was completely squashed. On the claim form in answer to the question about the cause of the accident, they read 'I was following a circus procession through the town, and it came to a railway bridge. At that moment, a train passed over the bridge, and this startled an elephant which was bringing up the rear of the procession. The elephant sat on the front of my car and that's why it's damaged.'

However, my informant's brother is also in the insurance business, and he avers that the elephant sat on the Mini because it mistook it for its circus tub. I remember the story was popular at about the time when the Mini came out (1960), and may have some foundation in the unprecedentedly revolutionary design at that time, just asking to be sat upon by elephants.

Sure enough, the elephant story had been circulating in the world of motor insurance before the time of the Mini, and the red Mini of the story, which reminded the sedentary pachyderm of its circus tub, was an example of the timeliness of the UL enjoying a Mini-revival.

Then there was the elephant who sat on (or possibly tried to mate with) a Mini, and died in the ensuing pile up. Fortunately, the police knew of a fat-rendering firm just off the motorway, and radioed them to ask if they took elephants. They said that they didn't, and in the end the elephant had to be buried out of public funds.

According to Grundy in *Punch*:

Elephants seem to be attracted to cars like bees to a honey-pot. A chap took his family to Knowsley Safari Park in South Lancashire. As they were driving around, an elephant got a bit uppity and bashed the car door. They didn't, of course, stop to reason with it, but drove off at high speed to the nearest bar, where the man downed a few swift ones to restore his shattered nerves. On the way home there was a three- or four-car 'shunt' ahead of them. Our man stopped for the vehicles to be got out of the way (nobody was hurt). As he sat there, a policeman came along and asked if he'd been involved in the accident. He replied, quite truthfully, that he hadn't. The policeman looked at the damaged car door and said: 'So how did this happen, then?' All unthinkingly the man replied: 'An elephant kicked it in.' The officer looked very hard at him and said: 'I think you'd better breathe into this bag, sir,' So he did. And he was over the limit.

Three weeks later, there was a follow-up:

A week or two ago I repeated the story of the man who had the door of his car kicked in by an elephant in a safari park . . . I was assured it was true, but doubted it. Now I get a letter from Robin Mackley which shows how wise my scepticism was. He says, and proves it, that he printed the story in the house journal of John Smith's Tadcaster Brewery as early as November 1976, and it wasn't Knowsley Park, Lancashire, but Flamingo Park, Yorkshire. How nice when one gets the truth at last. But wait . . . what have we here? A letter from Patricia Hess of London W8, who proves to me – What is proof? said jesting Pilate – that it happened years ago in New York . . .

While all this was going on, I heard the following story from several sources. A foaf drove into a safari park, and his wife ill-advisedly wound down her window for some fresh air – the next thing they knew was that an elephant's trunk was curling through the window in search of sandwiches. Mrs Foaf panicked, and wound up the window, catching the elephant's trunk. The entrapped beast, more in dismay than in anger, placed its front feet on the side of the car and pulled. It released its trunk, but dented the car, and the foaf had the problem of explaining the 'cause of accident' to the insurance company.

Two days later, I heard the story again, as follows: A foaf was driving through a safari park when he spotted a fellow-visitor whose car had broken down. He stopped to help, and because his wife was sitting in the car, opened the windows because it was stuffy. The wife and the elephant behaved as before, and the incident so shook the foaf that he had a stiff drink before setting off down the M6 for home. Noticing the somewhat damaged car, the motorway police gave chase, stopped it and sought an explanation. 'An elephant dented it,' explained the foaf, reeking of brandy. To cut short a story of quite sufficient length, he lost his licence.

There is something appealing about the elephant: its looks, its trunk, its smile, its docility *vis-à-vis* its size, the fact that man can bend it to his will – all these give one a feeling of companionship (not to mention a secret superiority). The elephant therefore has a special ethos of, for example, elephant jokes; the production of a set of jokes about anything is an accolade in itself.

But apart from 'why did the elephant paint his toenails red?' there are more serious tales concerning the astonishing memory of the elephant. This UL is of the hunter who somehow wounds a young elephant, which makes its escape. However, it turns up in a circus many years later, spies the hunter in the audience, lifts him out and revengefully tramples him to death. The alternative – not, presumably a UL – concerns the hunter's performing some service to the elephant – such as releasing it from a snare – and the elephant, spying him in the one-and-ninepennies at the circus, lifts him out and places him gently in the three-and-sixpennies (the Androcles syndrome). Those were the seat prices when I heard the tale.

Once more life has recently imitated art – or at any rate the world of advertising has assimiliated a UL: a boy taunts a baby elephant with some sweetmeat; years later the boy (now a man) is watching a circus parade, and the adult elephant takes its revenge with a well-placed blow of its trunk.

One more tale before I leave elephants. An old lady rings up the police in a state of great nervousness: 'Officer, there's a huge grey animal in my vegetable garden.'

'Oh yes, madam, and what's it doing?'

'It's trampling all over my cabbages and pulling them up with its tail.'

'With its *tail*, madam? And what's it doing with them then?'

'If I told you that, officer, you wouldn't believe me!'

I have heard it said that horses are attracted to humans (are they?) because their eyes distort their view of humans so that humans look like horses. However, a moment's thought will show that, in that case, a horse looking at another horse would see something else again . . . If horses like humans, it's because they know which side out their nosebags are.

A tale of the thoughtful rapport which we would all like to have with the animal kingdom (*cf* Dr Doolittle), is woven into the message of *Androcles and the Lion*. Androcles removes a thorn from the lion's paw, and the lion later rewards him by not eating him when, in his capacity as a Christian, he is thrown to it.

In a shaggy dog/folk-tale version, a mouse gnaws through a lion's bonds, and the grateful lion offers him any reward he cares to name. The mouse asks for the lion's daughter's hand in marriage. The wedding ceremony ends in mourning, when the bride accidentally steps on her groom.

The following story was told to me by the teacher to whom it happened: she was asked by one of her class how to spell 'vulture'. She imparted the necessary information, thinking to herself that at last she was going to see a really creative piece of work. When it was handed in, however, her delight changed its direction, for she read: 'I got a Boots Gift Vulture for Christmas . . .

Since we're back to birds, I will take the opportunity of recounting a UL in the making – it occurs in a review of *Animal World* (1977), wherein are found the following words:

There is also a special chapter on unsolved problems. Myths are debunked, but plenty of mysteries remain, such as; magpies' mass meetings; rooks who light matches and hold the flames under their wings . . .

This I had to explore, so I turned to the book in question. I was disappointed to find that the report was of a crow which liked to sit in the smoke of a straw fire in its aviary, though the operation was difficult, because as fast as a match was struck the excited crow would snatch it from one's fingers and hold it under its wing. In its 20 years, the crow fire-bathed hundreds of times.

It all sounds highly dangerous. And how, I wonder, does one discover that an animal likes taking part in such unusual activities? It is a sobering thought that if this is true practically every member of the animal kingdom – perhaps even of the plant kingdom – is awaiting in vain for such simple pleasures to be identified.

The techniques of book-reviewing are sobering, too.

My father was having some trouble with a blocked lavatory. He took his old-fashioned lavatory brush and broddled it up and down in the pan; then he looked in and – what should he see, but a hedgehog! 'Poor thing,' he thought, 'fancy falling into a lavatory and drowning.' then he looked at his lavatory brush, and found that, owing to the ravages of woodworm, the head had snapped off and was giving an erinaceous impression.

A foaf told me of a man who worked in an office upstairs from her, and had just received a telephone call from his wife asking him what to do about supper that night. She had left the kitchen door open after collecting the washing from the line, and then opened the oven door to check on the casserole within. As she took the lid from the dish, the smell attracted a passing rat, which ran into the kitchen and plunged greedily straight into the casserole. In shock, she had slammed down the lid on the dish, closed the oven door, and ran screaming down the road and into the nearest telephone kiosk, leaving the rat gently cooking in the stock.

A friend's uncle was a vet, who spent some time abroad in the Middle East. One day, he was walking through the streets when he heard a noise approaching him from behind – on inspection, it turned out to be a pack of rabid dogs coming after him. What should he do? With great presence of mind, he seized a stone from a wall and flung it at the leader of the pack. The leader was hit between the eyes and fell, whereupon the rest of the pack set upon the body, enabling the pursued to make his getaway.

The same tale is told of wolves in Russia; they chase after your sledge in a pack, and the technique is to shoot the leader. Its fellows fall on the body and devour it; this enables you to get ahead before they catch up with you again and you have to shoot another – and so on until you reach your destination.

A similar danger befell Baron Munchausen when he was walking the streets of St Petersburg and was assailed by a mad dog. The Baron ran towards home, taking off his fur cloak as he went; he cast the cloak down in the path of the dog, which instantly set upon it. Later, the Baron sent his servant for the cloak; it was retrieved and hung in the wardrobe. The next day, the Baron found that the cloak had become rabid and torn all the clothes in the wardrobe to pieces – how he dealt with it is not told.

It was on the way to St Petersburg on a one-horse sledge that the Baron suddenly spied a voracious wolf gaining on him. To put on speed, the Baron reduced his wind-resistance by lying flat but the wolf continued to gain on them. At last, with a great leap, the wolf sprang, but to the Baron's surprise it sailed over the sledge and took hold of the rear end of his horse. This made the horse run even faster, as the wolf ate its way into his body. Always ready to make capital out of his extraordinary adventures, the Baron whipped the wolf into the horse, the shell of the horse fell to the ground, the wolf found himself in the harness, and thus they arrived triumphant in St Petersburg.

While I'm on the subject of the Baron, I will recount one further singular phenomenon, though it has nothing to do with animals. You will have gathered that he was a great traveller and teller of tales, and he recalled an occasion when, travelling through the frozen wastes in his carriage, the postillion put his horn to his lips and attempted to play all manner of tunes – but the air was so cold that no sound came out.

Later that day, they took refuge in an inn for the night, the postillion placed his horn by the fire and, the instrument thawing out, all the tunes he had attempted to play earlier came out, and entertained the assembled company for some time.

Many of the baron's adventures, it should be pointed out, had already befallen earlier explorers.

Fishy stories from Baron Munchausen, a fishy story from Cornwall. While her husband was out in a boat sea-fishing, the wife, who was bathing, found to her consternation that she had lost her wedding-ring. Although she knew it to be fruitless, she searched for some times as one does, before returning to their rented cottage.

In due time, her husband returned home well pleased with his catch and started to prepare it for the table. He was told by his tearful wife of her loss, and was about to wash his hands to comfort her when he felt something inside the fish he was gutting. And do you know what? It was the lost wedding ring! What are the chances of that happening, eh?

Ripley tells a wedding-ring story:

Mrs A A Viel of Greytown, Natal, South Africa baked 150 cakes for the troops in Europe in 1941. She missed her wedding ring, so to save opening all the cakes she sent a note with them. The finder was – of all people – her son, Sgt Ronnie Viel, who by an extraordinary coincidence was handed one of the cakes in London and found his mother's ring in it.

Ripley also reports a watch in a fish, a crab wearing sunglasses, and a goldfish with a hawthorn tree growing out of its head. In another place he writes:

The editor of *The Torch* assures me that the following paragraph which appeared in his newspaper is nothing but the truth.

Seven years ago a farmer in Iowa hung his vest [waistcoat] on a fence in the barnyard. A calf chewed up a pocket in the garment in which was a gold watch. Last week the animal, a staid old milk cow, was butchered for beef, and the timepiece was found in such a position between the lungs of the cow that respiration – the closing in and filling of the lungs – kept the stem-winder wound up, and the watch had lost but four minutes in seven years.

While we're on staid old milk cows, here's one from a veterinary research laboratory. There was a man there who had a disembodied cow's udder as part of a piece of apparatus so arranged that when emulsified grass was fed in at one end, milk would come out of the udder. But the coincidence was that his wife – like Anne Boleyn – had a supernumerary breast . . .

9

Chop Chop

You see what will happen if
you keep on biting your nails.
*Noel Coward; Message on a
postcard of the Venus de Milo*

Why, one wonders, should anyone want to tell a story about some part of the human body being snipped, hacked or wrenched off? And why, once such a story has been told, should the listener want to retell it as his own? Superficially, our culture does not admit to our enjoying such tales, so why do they exist? It sees to me that, placed in context of the broader spectrum of the UL, their existence becomes more explicable.

One may conjecture that the more ghastly a story is, the more likely it is to be believed, since the teller is obviously (?) not telling it for fun. There is a need for the catharsis of telling others about an accident you have witnessed, or the death of someone, however remote the connection with you, and it may be that some people find the same vicarious pleasure in telling the ghastly UL. Some are rather like a particular sort of teenage joke to which those with teenagers are subjected at the appropriate stage of development, though I do not think that an urge to shock always lies beneath the telling of a ghastly UL.

Perhaps I ought to get on with some examples. If you don't feel strong enough, leave this chapter out. Remember, however, that having studied it you will be able to laugh in the face of anyone who tries to serve you one of the golden oldies.

The first incident happened in a village in North Wales, which shall be nameless, as there is only one butcher (Jones the Butcher) there and we don't want to get him a bad name. Jones the Butcher was famed for his sausages, and took a great pride in his spicy recipe, which had been handed down for many generations. Now, accidents happen in the best regulated butcheries, and one day a nest of mice somehow found its way into the mincing machine and – whoosh –

there it wasn't before you could say Steele-Bodger's XV. Jones the Butcher looked at the mince, and couldn't see any signs of the unwanted meat, so he shrugged his shoulders and made his batch of sausages – which, as usual, was sold almost as soon as it was ready. The following day, Mrs Morgan came into the shop: 'Would it be possible to have some more of those delicious sausages, Mr Jones? I've never tasted anything quite like them before.'

Before the war, a foaf and his friend were on a walking tour in the Black Forest. Somehow, they lost their way and began to feel rather worried as it began to get dark, for it was a very chilly evening. Luckily, they saw a light, and found a little cottage, smoke curling from the chimney in the approved fashion. They knocked on the door. It was opened by – guess who? – an old woodcutter: they were given an effusive welcome and ushered into the kitchen where there was a great cauldron steaming over an open fire. They were given large helpings of delicious stew, and hunks of freshly-made bread. After they had refreshed themselves, they learned that the place for which they were heading was not far away, and the woodcutter offered to show them the way. The offer was gratefully accepted and within the hour they were safe and sound at their hotel, and the woodcutter was back in his cottage with a suitable reward. When they were in the privacy of their room, the foaf could contain his curiosity no longer, and said to his friend: 'What was that you put in your pocket when we were eating the stew?' His friend pulled it out and they studied it in fascinated amazement: there was no doubt about it – it was definitely a human fingernail.

Some friends threw a party which was more of a success than they'd dared to hope. The food and drink was fast disappearing so the guests were invited into the kitchen to help themselves to more. The party went swingingly, then somebody discovered that what they had taken to be a baby gherkin lying in the pickles dish was in fact a human finger.

A foaf went into an Indian restaurant and ordered a chicken curry. When it came, he saw instantly that, though there were pieces of chicken-skin in the gravy, the meat itself was cat. How did he know? Well, he happened to be Professor of Veterinary Anatomy in the university.

Every university town has its Indian restaurant serving cats. ('We serve anybody, sir. Sit down.') If there isn't a chair of veterinary anatomy . . . well, there are always visiting professors. The foregoing has cropped up perpetually during my 50+ years of curry eating; I myself experienced an interesting variation.

Three of us went on the milk round to one of the larger Northern Universities; Robert, whose alma mater it was, assured Janet and me that, if we hadn't eaten at a certain Indian restaurant, we hadn't lived. It was with unrestrained eagerness that we allowed him to pilot us to the unforgettable eating-house – and we certainly haven't forgotten it. It stood in the middle of a site cleared for development, and we picked our way towards it: its lights shone out like a guiding beacon over the rubble. A 'waiter' with an unbelievably filthy overall pointed to the only table of the two which was vacant. It was fastened to the ground, as were the stools – presumably the delicate balance of the layout would have been upset if clients had dared to move the furniture. The menu was written up on a blackboard, and there were in effect nine dishes: chicken, meat or egg; hot, medium or mild. I ordered hot egg, and waited to see what would happen. It came in a battered aluminium bowl rather like a trumpet mute along with a plate of rice. In the bowl was some very hot curry gravy; a fried egg floating on the top, and some cabbage leaves underneath. It was very tasty, and the three of us feasted for a sum too little to have fed only one at any normal restaurant. When we had finished, our proud demonstrator said: 'There's a very interesting story I heard about that place.' We couldn't wait. 'During my last year here, their deep-freeze was found to be full of alsatian carcasses. The public health people tried to prosecute, but the restaurant was offering "meat", and alsatian is "meat", so they got away with it.'

Such is the process of law – at least in UL. Subsequently, I heard the tale in two other northern towns.

Without letting on that we'd been there, Janet and I asked one of our interviewees the following day if he knew of the place. 'God, yes,' he replied. 'There's a story about a student here who ate there every day, and at the end of his three years he had to go into hospital to have his guts rebuilt.'

Not that Indian restaurants are the only ones where odd things happen. A foaf was the wife of a sometime British Consul in Hong Kong. Apparently, she had there gone into a Chinese restaurant with her little poodle, been ushered to a table, and indicated that she would like her dog to be fed as well. The inscrutable waiter took the dog to the inner regions, and in due time it was returned to its mistress as a succulent dish, dressed like a sucking-pig with its bejewelled collar in its mouth.

Chows were, of course bred for eating, which may be the origin of this story. Rob B-J, ex-pat QS, found it impossible to forgive his Korean employees when he saw dogs being taken to the kitchens – to be despatched with a 'Dong – Aaagh', presumably. But of course it is well known that on Polar expeditions the Huskies are made use of as meat, so this UL has a genuine pedigree.

On the one hand, eating dogs isn't 'civilised'. But why not? They eat horses, don't they? What about guinea-pigs? Why can I eat prawns and crabs, but draw the line at witchety grubs? It must be a question of need; I'm sure the goalposts would be move pretty rapidly if one were starving . . . horses for courses.

Cats in Indian restaurants? Is it true that Indians eat Kit-e-Kat? Why not, it's quite wholesome, though nowadays it's not PC to suggest that they do, any more than that they are not too good at electrical installation. Where does fact end and fiction begin? There was the famous restaurant that apparently served rat as a delicacy. There is more than one case of a prosecution for having live chickens in the kitchen. In Arab – and no doubt other – countries, there are shops devoted to selling chickens, killed while you wait, with bins outside where you can find heads, entrails, *etc.*

So, a few notes on chickens. A foaf was feeding some chickens on behalf of a friend of his, who was away on holiday. The foaf was particularly upset by one of the birds, which would keep pecking his legs. Eventually, he took up the nearest thing to hand (which happened to be a billhook) and threw it at the importunate bird. Although the bird was decapitated, it ran around for fully five minutes.

Five minutes? Not very long. On 14 November 1904, one Herbert V Hughes, the proprietor of the Belvedere Hotel of Sault Ste Marie, Michigan, was killing chickens for Sunday dinner in the usual way. His kitchen maid was picking and cleaning them, when suddenly she fled screaming in terror. A black Minorcan chicken was walking slowly round the room. The problem was that it was headless! The hen refused to die, and naturally attracted much publicity, drawing crowds to the Belvedere Hotel. Mr Hughes fed the chicken by means of a syringe 'injected into the raw end of the food pipe'. The hen would walk about, flap her wings, and go through the motions of stretching up and smoothing her feathers just as though her head were still there. At other times she would turn on her perch, sit down and get up and turn again, and at other times tried to croak or sing. She appeared not to suffer pain and to be as happy and contented as any hen.

> The chicken lived until 30 November, seventeen days after her head was cut off, and might have lived longer but for the fact that a 'careless attendant' allowed the end of her neck to heal over the end of the windpipe and choke her to death.

> Careless indeed, since the hen was clearly a first-class draw (!) for the Belvedere Hotel.

Ripley's story of the Belvedere chicken is accompanied by two more. Mr Wm Hinkleman, who lives in California, states:

> Many years ago on a ranch near Modesto I cut the head completely off a chicken and the chicken lived over a year. It was fed by a tube inserted in its neck and was on exhibition for some time in San Francisco.

That one probably died of boredom. Another account was afforded by Mrs Mary Jane Beerup:

> My father was killing and dressing a chicken for a country fair when he discovered one that he thought he had killed walking around with its head off. I fed it through its neck for several days and it is no telling how long it would have lived had it not caught its neck on a splinter and bled to death . . .

Tut, tut. Another careless attendant. Recently the production of chickens has increased enormously, and yet the number of headless ones strutting around appears to have dropped. But there will doubtless continue to be reports of them.

A classic UL tells of an extraordinary incident on the East Lancs Road (A580). Apparently, a motorcyclist was riding behind a lorry that was carrying a load of thin steel plates. He decided to overtake the lorry, but as he moved out towards the centre of the road, one of the steel sheets became dislodged and decapitated him. However, his momentum carried him alongside the lorry, the lorry-driver glanced from his window, saw the headless motorcyclist passing, had a heart attack, ran off the road and was killed.

The headless motorcyclist is, perhaps, a modern version of the headless horseman. Perhaps the original headless horseman was Shah Ghazi Kaml of Bahu, Punjab, India. He lost his head in the battle of Jhajjar in 1635, but he did not sink lifeless from the saddle – his body was so securely seated that his trusty steed carried him home – a distance of some 26 miles. His body was lifted reverently from the saddle and placed in an ornate tomb – later a mosque and an artificial lake were added, and pilgrims have been visiting the place ever since.

It was back in the 1950s that a foaf was chased by a gang of teddy-boys while he was walking late one night along the promenade at Folkestone. Luckily, his car was not far away and he was an athletics Blue, so he sprinted for the vehicle, got in, started the engine and drove away ahead of his pursuers. He heard an almighty BANG on the body, and there was a bit of a jerk, but he got safely away. When he arrived home, he got out to inspect the damage, and there was a bicycle chain with a finger trapped in it. He went to the police, and via the hospital service they were able to trace the gang and take them to court.

This foaf was not the only one who has suffered such an attack. Another, in somewhat similar circumstances, managed to get away in his Volkswagen in the nick of time, but on this occasion the finger was trapped in the engine-grille at the rear. Another foaf was set upon in the Cambridge Lion Yard multi-storey car park, again managed to get away, but found a thumb stuck in the car door on arriving home – or so it was averred by the magistrate who told me of it in hushed tones.

However, all these incidents are trivial compared with another foaf who managed to reach his car, but couldn't get away in time. The thugs rocked the car, and banged on the roof, and lifted it up by the rear bumper. But they made a mistake: it was a front-wheel drive and the foaf was able to get away with some struggle. When he inspected the damage, he found a hand caught under the bumper. Of course, he went to the police and they made extensive enquiries, but after some weeks there was no news. They advised him to forget all about it.

It happens in America as well, and it may be that the subject of the next story is the same as he in the last. The foaf at last managed to fix a date with a girl he'd admired from afar for some time; they visit a movie, and then go for a car-ride, pull off the road, turn off the lights and find some sweet music on the radio. However, just as things are

starting to happen, the sweet music is interrupted for a news flash about an escaped sex-maniac with a hook hand. Now this upsets the girl greatly because she has visions of the man coming to get them, and nothing the foaf can say will persuade her otherwise, so he agrees to take her home. The car seems to be stuck in the mud, but he revs up and manages to get on to the highway and takes her home. He goes round to open the door for her and there, hanging on the handle, is a hook . . .

A friend of mine was told of the same species of experience by two other people; one said that it had happened in this country and the other that it had happened in Italy. It seems that in each case the girl was motoring with her boyfriend, when the car ran out of petrol. It was late at night, but they had passed an all-night garage not far back, and he had a can with him, so he decided to walk back. The girl locked the doors and curled up on the back seat. She was rudely awoken by someone rocking the car and banging on the roof. This went on and on – she huddled under a blanket too frightened to do anything. The interference stopped as abruptly as it started, and she dropped into an uneasy and uncomfortable sleep. Then she was awoken by more knockings and shouts of 'Open up, Police!'. Having warily ascertained that it was indeed the police, she opened the door, and allowed herself to be carried away. Later she found that her boyfriend had never left the vicinity; outside the car he had been set upon by a madman who had decapitated him, using the vehicle as an operating table.

There are worse versions. In another, the boyfriend is decapitated and hung from a tree over the car, and it is his shoes which go 'bang, bang, bang' on the car roof all night. And sometimes the decapitated body is hung upside-down . . . (drip, drip).

Sometimes, the decapitation takes place in a university hall of residence: frightened girls are huddled in a room while horrific noises are heard outside. In the morning, the decapitated body is found in the passage.

Or again, a girl gets home late from a dance, and doesn't discover until morning that her room-mate – who didn't go to the dance, and whom she thought was asleep when she arrived home – has in fact been mutilated in her bed. Or worse still, the bloodthirsty maniac was actually hiding in the room when the latecomer returned. And sometimes, she turns on the light and discovers him behind the door with a bloody axe. The rationale of these stories is surely wonderful to consider.

A most unfortunate incident occurred last year (and the year before, and the year before that). In fact there ought to be pressure for a ban on Guy Fawkes, as on fireworks. It seems that to meet the increasing competition for bigger and better guys, a group of boys dressed one of their number in suitable clothes and installed him in the cart. As they processed along the High Street, they came to a butcher's shop, and crowded in with the inflationary demand '5p for the guy'. The butcher, however, had been plagued with such demands and, taking up a sharp knife, laid into the 'effigy', stabbing it repeatedly. The charge, of course, was manslaughter.

A girl was baby-sitting for three small children in a quiet, secluded house. At about 11 o'clock – long before the parents were expected back – she was awakened from her armchair doze by a telephone call. She answered it, but the caller had nothing to say; he just laughed softly to himself. So she replaced the receiver, turned up the television, and tried to forget about it. About 10 minutes later he phoned again. This time he laughed more loudly, more menacingly; she slammed down the receiver and felt very scared. So she called the operator and asked her to trace the call. Needless to say, he phoned again – this time his laughter was hysterical, demonic. She threw down the phone and in the next instant the operator called her back. 'We've traced the call, said the operator, 'it seems to be coming from your upstairs extension . . . ' And even as she spoke the manic laughter grew louder, and the door handle slowly turned . . .

  In other versions of this tale the murderer actually tells the baby-sitter that he has killed the children, but the girl thinks it's a hoax. And in another tale, there are two baby-sitters, one of whom goes to tend to the children and surprises the madman just as he's finishing them off. Downstairs, the operator calls back; the other girl rushes upstairs to see what's going on, to be met by her friend, with all limbs severed from her body, pulling herself down the stairs with her chin – bump, bump, bump, bump.

As if children don't have enough to fear from nocturnal prowlers, there's the added menace of infanticidal baby-sitters.

  A couple asked some friends if their student daughter would like to babysit for them one evening and earn herself some pocket money. She arrived with her rather unsavoury-looking boyfriend and the couple went off to their dinner party. In the middle of the evening the father phoned home to see if everything was okay. 'Sure,' drawled the girl, 'we're getting along just fine. I've just finished stuffing the turkey and we've put it in the oven right now. Everything's out of sight. Don't worry.' He passed on the message to his wife who didn't like the sound of it at all, especially when she remembered that they didn't have a turkey. They made their excuses and rushed home, arriving just in time to see the spaced out sitters taking their roast baby from the oven.

A woman engaged in research in Nigeria employed a local girl to look after her house and baby while she was away at work. The girl arrived and seemed willing enough, if a little overawed. So in the middle of the morning the woman phoned to ensure that she and the baby were getting along okay. The girl told her that the baby was still in bed, but when the mother told her to get him up, she reluctantly agreed. That evening, when the woman returned home she could see that the girl was most upset about something. 'You can tell me,' she said 'it can't be all that bad. Bring me my son and we'll talk about it over supper.' Red-eyed the girl went into the kitchen and returned with the baby. Now what the mother hadn't realised was that in Efit, the words *men eyen oro k'etem* can mean two things, either 'sit the baby up' or 'cook the baby'. And she could only stare in horrified disbelief at the roasting dish laid on the dinner table before her.

A Norwegian couple, who had not had a proper holiday for years, decided to treat themselves to a long, winter holiday in the sun. At last the great day dawned; everything was packed and loaded into the car – as soon as Nanny arrived they could away. But today of all days, Nanny was late. At the last minute she phoned and told them that her car had broken down. The man said that if they came to collect her now they would miss their flight; was it too far to walk? Nanny said it wasn't; they could leave and she'd be there in a quarter of an hour. So the wife strapped their young son into his highchair, told him Nanny wouldn't be long and set off for their island in the sun. During the long, hot weeks away they missed the news that the Nanny had been hit by a lorry and killed on her way to their house. When at last they returned, sun-bronzed and rejuvenated, they found the remains of their starved son still strapped into his chair where they had left him.

A foaf went up to his retreat in the mountains for a long weekend; on the Saturday morning he is awoken by raging toothache. By this time the roads are blocked with snow, but then he remembers that the man in the neighbouring cabin about half-a-mile away is a dentist . . . is he there? The phone lines are down, so he wraps up warmly and sets off, every step setting his tooth a-throbbing. Luckily the dentist is in residence, spots the foaf approaching and goes out to meet him – yes, he *has* got some instruments; he'll see what he can do. Well, of course, there's a shortage of anaesthetic, but plenty of whisky, and soon the foaf is strapped into a sturdy chair, and out to the world. The dentist gets the offending tooth half out . . . and collapses from a fatal heart attack.

A man arrived home, somewhat inebriated, and fell asleep on the sofa. His wife had long since retired to bed but their two teenage sons were still out. When they eventually returned home they found their father in a drunken sleep and decided to play a joke on him. They took a turkey neck and placed it inside his trouser flies with the end protruding. The father slept through all this and the two sons, feeling rather pleased with themselves, went upstairs to bed. The next morning, when the wife went downstairs to make a pot of tea, she saw her husband soundly sleeping on the sofa – and the family cat hungrily gnawing on the turkey neck. She fainted with shock and suffered severe scalds.

A foaf spent a busy evening playing with a newly-acquired and very playful kitten. Then, ready for bed, he changed into his pyjamas, but decided to watch just one more frame of snooker on the television; however, he fell asleep. When he awoke, he realised he should be in bed, and knelt down to switch off the set. As he did so, the kitten espied his genitals through his pyjama flies and, mistaking them for a new plaything, sprang towards them, sinking in claws and teeth on arrival. The friend leapt with pain and in so doing thrust his head through the television screen. He never did find out who had won the game.

At the beginning of the war, a young mother sailed for Ireland with her two young children, a girl of five and a baby of two. She was trying to settle them in their bunks for the night so that she could go off for dinner, but the baby refused to stop crying. In desperation, she shouted: 'If you don't shut up, I'll put you out of the porthole.' This seemed to quiet the child, and she went for her meal. When she returned, the porthole was open, the baby was gone, and her daughter slept blissfully.

For our closing story, there is another harassed mum with two children: the small boy – who is making a nuisance of himself – and the larger girl. This time, she shouts: 'If you don't go to sleep I'll . . . I'll . . . cut off your willie.' This threat seems to work, so she goes down stairs and relaxes with a suitable glass. Then – there is a scream from withup, and she rushes to the foot of the stairs to be greeted with her angelic daughter, brandishing a pair of dressmaking scissors, saying: 'He didn't keep quiet, so I cut it off for you.' To the hospital quickly! Mum grabs him from the cot, wraps him in a blanket and rushes down stairs, shouting to her daughter: 'You'd better come with me so that I can keep an eye on you.' She runs out to the garage, opens the doors and lays her son on the back seat of the car. Then she climbs in, reverses out of the garage, and runs over her daughter.

The Silver Jubilee of the Foaf

An edited version of a paper presented by the author to the 20th ISCLR (International Society for Contemporary Legend Research) Conference, Sheffield University, 24 July 2002.

As a salutary reminder to us all, I will begin by quoting that extraordinary man Samuel Johnson: 'There are two things I can do very well: one is an introduction to any literary work, stating what it is to contain, and how it should be executed in the most perfect manner: the other is a conclusion, shewing from various causes why the execution has not been equal to what the authour promised to himself and to the publick.'

I promise that there will be some points of contact between my abstract and what I am about to say, but the rest might be labelled *Apologia Johnsoniensis*, and I'm sure that this state of affairs holds for anyone who ever wrote the abstract before considering what he or she was going to say – which is just about everybody, everywhere, everywhen.

There is something spuriously magic about numbers ending in 0. In recent years we've all noted the growing tendency for people to decorate roundabouts and the like with bunches of balloons accompanying ill-limned sheets of cardboard wrested from some discarded cornflakes box inviting the passer-by to 'Guess who's 40 today'. Why not 'Guess who's 37 today'? I took part in the first ISCLR Conference in 1982 and, because of the strange aura surrounding numbers divisible by 10, I felt an urge to speak at the 20th ISCLR Conference.

Just as the identification and development of the craft of the urban legend sprang into being simultaneously and independently at several places in the 70s – and anything I say is open to correction – it now seems that at least some of those involved simultaneously and independently feel a need to record what happened in those early days before memories, already rapidly deteriorating, are lost for ever.

There is of course a danger that the activity might become a bit anorak, comparable with captions to photographs of The 'Jubilee' Class 5XP 4-6-0 Tender No 5688 *Polyphemus* forming the 8.23 from Penzance steaming up the Wheal Margaret incline (1:462) on 24 May 1951 with Arthur Shuttleworth at the regulator and Tom Dickson firing.

When I first met a consciously-identified urban legend, it was a 'whale-tumour story'. And like some old fogey who uses such words as aerodrome and wireless I have continued to think of ULs as whale-tumour stories, or WTSs. I hope this won't worry anyone; rather that it will bring a quaint, old-fashioned air to the proceedings.

I'll begin by telling you how I got into this business. Much of what follows may be found in my books – particularly in *The Tumour in the Whale* – but since it would be big-headed of me to assume that anyone has read what I've written – let alone remembered it – let me go over the story, hoping that those whom I have misjudged on those counts will bear with me, remembering that the music-hall audiences of yore hated the artistes to change their acts, because familiarity enables one to belong to the in-group of those who know what's coming next.

My story begins on a hot July evening in 1976; George Melly was to perform with John Chilton and the Feetwarmers in Cambridge Guildhall, and we had met beforehand in the yard of the Eagle Tavern in Bene't Street, Cambridge. We talked; George described some anecdote as a 'whale-tumour story', a synechdochial description of its genre – as in 'shaggy dog story' – where the characteristic of one example becomes the title for all. The story in question went as follows: 'During the War, when whale-meat was offered as a substitute for beef, a woman bought some whale steak, took it home, and put it on a plate on the kitchen dresser. Her husband was sitting in the adjacent living room, when suddenly a movement in the kitchen caught his eye . . . on investigation, they found that the whale steak contained a live tumour, gently throbbing.'

We fell to discussing the whale-tumour genre – the way in which you hear a story that the teller swears is true, in that it happened to a friend (or a friend of a friend, or a second cousin of the man who comes to mend the washing machine) and suddenly you hear the same story from many different people, up and down the country. Later, as I sat and thought about it, I recalled a number of such stories I'd heard over the years, and this led me to write an article for the Christmas 1976 number of Cambridge Consultants' house-magazine *Interface*, in those days a vehicle for many a pioneering venture, both technical and literary, and one of whose consultant editors I happened to be at the time.

My article – 'A Tumour in the Whale' – contained first a note of various types of story, then some analysis of the possible reasons for the popularity of the WTS, and finally some of the WTSs themselves.

The standfirst of the article is interesting, as I presented a different version of the protoWTS: 'The family sat down to a great steaming whale-liver pie – the treat of the week in those dreary war years. The pie was on the sideboard, waiting to be served. Suddenly, they noticed that it seemed to be throbbing rhythmically. Mum opened the crust gingerly, and investigated further. There, in the whale liver, was a live tumour . . . '

Presumably the story dated back to the heyday of whale meat during the War, and was a naughty attempt to put people off. I should say that on a Norwegian cruise earlier this year – the Hurti-gruten for those who know what I mean – I had a whale steak and it was delicious – and not a tumour to be seen.

In the *Interface* article I mentioned the 'friend of a friend' to whom things happen, but did not use the word 'foaf'. This emerged when I began to write my book the following year – 1977 – and that is why I claim that the year 2002 is the Silver Jubilee of the Foaf.

As well-known genres of story, I mention in the article the Shaggy Dog, the Ghost Story, and the Old Wives' Tale – and now the Whale-Tumour Story. I didn't at that time include – as Richard Dorson did in his foreword to Briggs & Tongue's *Folktales of England* of 1963 – I didn't include jokes, tall tales and numskull [sic] stories, but I had not then come across Briggs & Tongue. However, Dorson does mention these as 'varieties of oral humour' saying that they 'abound among educated city folk.' He goes on to say that 'little attempt has yet been made to gather and examine these forms' (apart from Partridge's analysis *The Shaggy Dog Story*). He adds: 'macabre legends also thrive in the modem metropolis' and goes on to describe the story of the stolen corpse – aka the granny on the roof-rack – as a 'modern legend'. I will return to the use of that description later.

My analysis of the WTS was that it is not purely a joke; if there is any humour it is that of relief. The teller wishes to be taken seriously and therefore (1) he affects to know – albeit remotely – to whom it happened and (2) the story is often unpleasant or macabre. Why does anyone want to tell a WTS? For the same reason that anyone wants to tell someone else anything, with the added urge to spread – and the frisson attendant upon spreading – what is, in effect, bad news. In addition, of course, we who are naturally modest perhaps find it easier to tell of a friend's demise than of our having been awarded an OBE.

The stories in the *Interface* article were as follows and, since we're playing anoraks, I will, for the record, give their provenance – and a bit of postvenance – as far as I'm concerned. I take it you'll all recognise them from my abbreviated descriptions. We haven't quite reached the stage, I fear, where I can say 'Number 83' and you'll all know the story.

1   *'If you don't shut up, I'll cut off your willy' says the exasperated mum; he didn't shut up so his little sister obliges; mum puts the abbreviated toddler in the car to rush him to hospital, but in backing out of the garage runs over her daughter.* I gleaned this in the 70s from a good friend, East Anglian Hospital Board architect Deric Platt. I can see his utter belief in the story – real or feigned – even now. The way the story builds up is obviously whale-tumoury, but in real life it is nevertheless all too frequent that the young and the old do get run over, particularly by deodand vehicles with automatic transmission, and farm tractors. *[Only last week, life tragically imitated art once again.]*

2   *The beehive hairstyle that was found to be full of maggots.* I heard this from Shenton Smith, a printer who worked for me, in about 1962. His sister was a hairdresser working in the very salon, he said, where it happened – though not, you will note, the hairdresser herself.

3   *The rash caused by lice in the waistband of a skirt imported from the Far East.* My mother told me this in all seriousness in about 1973 – it happened to a friend of hers, whom she refused to name on the grounds that I 'might go questioning her'.

4   *The police car that elected to test the brakes of an old jalopy by driving behind it and sounding the horn as a signal to stop whereupon, the jalopy's brakes being more powerful than you'd think, the police car ran into the back of it.* I was a post-war vintage motorist, and this tale went round our circle in the early 50s. Subsequently, when I was a Cambridge City magistrate (appointed 1976), I was on the bench that tried a traffic policeman for careless driving in somewhat similar circumstances. The vehicle to be tested was a Reliant

Robin, and one of the policemen sat in the back seat with a Tapley meter, while the other followed in the police car. The horn sounded, the brakes were applied, and the cop in the Robin went head over heels into the front seat well. Life imitates art again. There was as much laughter in court that day as on another occasion when a young solicitor was applying for a liquor licence for a new eatery to be called Colonel Fudpucker's.

5 *The shark slicing through the surfboard.* This came from an old friend – Elna Forsyth of Parson's Green – in 1975. I can even now hear her protesting its truth. 1975 was, by some coincidence, the year in which the film Jaws was released. *[Again life imitated art in 2003 when champion surfer Bethany Hamilton lost her left arm to a shark; I am assured that the surfboard illustrated on the jacket of her book is 'the very one', but find the spatial relationship of the parts attacked difficult to envisage.]*

6 *The kitten travelling in the long-haul locomotive firebox, or on the connecting rod.* There is a less WTS-y version of this in *Speeding North with the 'Royal Scot'* (1939), where the kitten travels among the coals in the locomotive tender. Kittens – or even cats – you will have noted, are from time to time found in the engine compartments of motor cars. Last year came the report of the young lady whose brand-new Land Rover had to be dismantled piece by piece to release her inadvertent hamster. *[And recently Freddy down the road, lost, was found under the bonnet of Mags's car.]*

7 *The £5 car (in which the vendor's husband committed suicide, or which she is selling to give her estranged spouse the proceeds).* This was another tale that went round the motoring fraternity in the early 50s. Certainly about that time Alec Popple – well mindful of the tale – screwed up the courage to reply to an unbelievable advertisement in the *Cambridge Evening News* offering a VW Beetle for £5 . . . at last he telephoned, and the price turned out to be a misprint.

8 *The Rolls-Royce crankshaft (or half-shaft) replaced for free on grounds that 'Rolls-Royce crankshafts never break, Sir'.* This was another vintage motoring story of the late 40s/early 50s. In about 1968 Peter Bill, managing director of Bill Switchgear, had heard – and believed – the tale when his Rolls broke down on the M1. He phoned Derby. 'I should go to a garage, if I were you, Sir,' said man. 'Hey, what about the crankshaft that broke in Spain?' protested Peter, recalling the WTS as true. 'We can send a mechanic if you wish, Sir, but it'll cost you £100 a day. I should go to a garage if we were

you.' At a guess that's now a few thousand pounds a day.

9   *The sports car erroneously filled with concrete*. I have to confess that
so far I have been unable to remember where I first heard this.

10 *Curried cat*. Curry was well established in Cambridge by 1955
and the story of the Professor of Veterinary Anatomy went with
it. I can remember exactly where I was sitting in the Kismet when
I heard the tale from my then flatmate Christopher Cook with
whom I played in *The New Orleans Jassmen* in 1956 *[along with
cornettist Dud Clews.]*

11 *The pet poodle served at table*. This was told to me by the editor of
Interface when we were discussing the article; together we served
the animal 'dressed like a sucking pig with its bejewelled collar in
its mouth.'

12 *The laughing paramedics, or ambulance men as they were then, who
dropped the patient with the lavatorially acid-splashed bum from their
stretcher and broke his leg*. I first heard this from the cartoonist Bill
Tidy, who illustrated the *Interface* article, and later *The Tumour
in the Whale*.

13 The misunderstood gynaecologist saying to the Indian
Ambassador's wife: 'Please lie on the couch', she replying
'Oh no . . . I want an Indian baby'. This too came from
Christopher Cook in about 1955; he swore that he knew the
Harley Street practitioner to whom it had happened.

*   *   *

If I may digress here, let me remind you of recent reports of the mix
up at the NHS fertility clinic which came to light when the babies
turned out (or emerged) the 'wrong' colour, whereupon a spokesman
at the clinic commented: 'Great steps have been taken to ensure that
this sort of thing never happens.' But he had the grace to add: 'It must
be a one in a million chance.' Most babies have emerged the 'correct'
colour, and in such cases nobody, I'm sure, has checked to make sure
that they have the 'correct' parents.

It must be true that, whatever precautions you take against this or
that possibility resulting in a particular undesired outcome, there will
always be something – perhaps many things – you haven't thought of.
Take the case reported on 11 July of the rare orchids at Came Down
near Dorchester. Conservationists had been nurturing a site of the
increasingly rare bee orchids and pyramid orchids for over 20 years.

They put up protective warning signs. The man on the mower had a detailed map *and* satellite navigation equipment so that 'nothing could possibly go wrong'. And yet he managed to mow round the sign and over the orchids, destroying 25 years' cherishing. If you can't prevent simple things like that happening, what chance have you against someone whose intentions are evil?

When will people realise that it is not in the nature of things to be perfect – were it so, Gaussian distribution curves would have blunt ends. No one – cabinet minister, scientist or publicity merchant – should ever think – let alone trumpet – that 'nothing can possibly go wrong'.

To underline what I'm saying, I read on Monday that Nick Irwin, deputy mayor of Sudbury, and chairman of Sudbury in Bloom, thought to tidy up a rough patch of grass just before the judges came round and – would you believe it? – he thus destroyed a patch of wild bee orchids which could many years to bloom again.

While I'm here, may I mention archaeological specimens which, to the team who unearthed them, are 'in a perfect state of preservation' – because of the ice, peat, dry atmosphere or whatever it might be in which they have lain for thousands of years? Unfortunately, when *I* look at such specimens, the archaeologists' idea of 'perfect preservation' seems to differ radically from mine . . . but perhaps to a discipline that can reconstruct a whole animal from a fragment of bone, or a whole city out of half a brick, this is not surprising.

My last shard of received wisdom is that any young person who dues unnaturally is always top of the class, academically brilliant, extremely popular among his (or her) fellows, would do anything for anybody, and with a bright future ahead (as if a future – bright or otherwise – could be anywhere else). We know that 'in lapidary inscriptions a man is not upon oath', but if you scan the detail of the often harrowing news items dealing with such topics, you'll see what I mean. If, by chance, the departure is seen as a good riddance, the subject will no doubt be described as a 'lovable rogue'.

Other popular misconceptions whose acceptance would save an enormous amount of time are that every question has an answer, and that every problem has a solution. I mention these matters because, to my mind the forces that myceliate the granny on the roof-rack are the big siblings of those that numb our centres of questioning when it comes to received wisdom.

This brings me to a point that I made more than a quarter of a century ago – will all this WTS activity put a stop to the stories? As more and more people became 'in the know'. Would they laugh at those who told the tales, exposing them for what they were? I didn't think so; persistent tellers would continue to assert that they knew that their tale was true, even though they were aware of all the others that weren't. Time has proved me right.

I'd better return to the 1976 *Interface* article, out of which I think I've squeezed the pips.

My purpose in writing it was not only to entertain the readers; I wanted also to find a publisher for a whole WTS book, and a published article confers a spurious authority on a project; it worked, and the following year I signed a contract with W H Allen for a paperback to be published under – or perhaps over – the Universal imprint. Knowing a masterpiece when he saw it, my late lamented friend Colin Haycraft of the publishing house Duckworth came to an arrangement with W H Allen to simultaneously publish – and that's not a split infinitive because it's a compound verb (an argument you can always adduce to silence barrack-room grammarians) – to simultaneously publish a hardback version of the book. Apart from the imprint, and the type size, the two versions differ only in the spelling on the front cover, in that the Duckworth shoutline describes the book as 'an hilarous collection of apocryphal anecdotes', a mistake that for ever more mortified the meticulous Colin when, in proudly passing me a copy of the book hot from the press, his eye suddenly fell on the misprint on the jacket.

Some copies, I believe, subsequently had a strip of opaque red tape stuck over the offending shoutline, but it was difficult to get the tape straight and it served only to draw attention to an error that otherwise went generally unnoticed.

The only attempt to publicise *Tumour* that I can remember resulted in my talking to Richard Robbins on LBC late one night in 1978, which reunited me with an old friend just returned from South Africa who happened to turn on the wireless at that moment. Some years later I was invited to join Robert Robinson and other guests on *Stop the Week*, where I was unprepared for the unlimited champagne and, to my shame, probably took more sips than I uttered words.

In 1982, Paul Smith invited me to the first WTS Conference in the Centre for English Cultural Tradition at Sheffield – 'Perspectives on Contemporary Legend'. I attended a 'meet the author' session on the afternoon of Friday 16 July, sharing the platform with Jan Harold

Brunvand. _The Vanishing Hitchhiker_ had been published the previous year; its blurb stated that it was 'the first book to discuss all the major American urban legends.' I remember little about the occasion, save that I was somewhat surprised to find that what I had thought was my light-hearted book was being taken somewhat seriously, and that everyone seemed very earnest, treating me and my book with a mixture of reverence and envy. But it was, of course, the first ever book to discuss WTSs as such. One audience comment was that 'we all sit around talking about writing books, and you've actually got on and done it. I think that there were more folklorists than tumourists present – understandable in those days.

Where did the stories in _Tumour_ come from? Many of them surfaced from the depths of my memory as I began to get into the task, writing them on sheets of card for later arrangement into some sort of order – the way that we worked in those days. I discussed the work with friends, almost all of whom had some contribution to make. There were 88 names in my acknowledgements list, some of whom yielded stories in discussion; others whose earlier stories I recalled when I put my mind to it.

When I think about it, it's clear that I have always questioned what I'm told, always quick to argue – sometimes annoyingly – with anyone who appears to be talking palpable nonsense. My book-shelves reflect this, and favourite volumes include Ripley's _Omnibus Believe it or Not_ (1935), Bergen Evans's _Natural History of Nonsense_ (1947) and _The Spoor of Spooks_ (1955), and H Allen Smith's _Compleat Practical Joker_ (1954). All these afforded WTS material, and triggers for WTS memories. Other books consulted are listed in _Tumour_ although Clyde Dawe's _Tumours in Aquatic Mammals_ (1976), is there only because it's too good to be true. (I've suddenly thought – suppose it were a collection of whale-tumour stories, and no one in our fraternity has cottoned on. Someone should investigate.)

In other circles, _The Tumour in the Whale_ had stirred up mass apathy, and by the time of the 1982 Sheffield Conference it was almost unobtainable. Some people – including Colin Haycraft – thought that would-be buyers might have been put off the book by the title and the drawing on the cover, so I contracted to produce a second book for Duckworth – _It's True, it Happened to a Friend_. Eventually, although illustrated by a friend of Colin's, _It's True_ turned out to sport a drawing on the cover even more off-putting than that on _Tumour_, sadly enabling me eventually to acquire the entire remaindered stock. *It's True*, by the way, doesn't use the word 'foaf' because Colin didn't like neologisms; it is, however, mentioned *en passant*. It also has the rare distinction of having been translated into Swedish of all tongues (*Det är sant . . . en god vän berättade*).

If anyone has any ideas for the disposal of unlimited copies of *It's True*, please let me know. I get the occasional request via e-mail, and send off a copy asking in return for euros or dollar bills. Some recipients don't bother to send the euros or dollar bills – such is the shortcoming of my faith in human nature.

Now, continuing in anorak mode, I'm going to look at the emergence of the term 'urban legend'. Brunvand used it in 1981, but as far as I can see, Paul Smith doesn't use the term in his *Book of Nasty Legends* (1983). The following year, It's True had the shout-line: 'A Collection of Urban Legends' without any 'apology quotes', so the term 'urban legend' was obviously established by then. What do the dictionaries say? My *OED* supplement (1987) makes no mention of urban anythings, nor of legends in the present sense, but under 'myth' it gives two interesting citations. 1963 *Brit Jnl Sociol* XIV 27: 'We use myth in a sense a little different from the popular one. To us it does not mean an untrue or impossible tale, but a tale that is told to justify some aspect of social order or of human experience.' In 1973, the Times 13 Nov 6/6: 'There is a myth going round that there are an awful lot of empty houses in Windsor Great Park.' A little tame, perhaps, but definitely whale tumoury, and somewhat reminiscent of the Paki-filled roofspaces of Bradford (*New Society* 22 September 1976).

In 1990 *The Longman Dictionary of New Words* (Volume 2) gives: '**foaf** *noun* a story passed on from one person to another several times, until it achieves the status of an urban legend.' (This implies that the story itself is a foaf. Shurely shome mishtake?) The entry then cites the *Sunday Times* 25 March 1990: 'Where do all the Foafs come from? Stories come from older stories, says Brunvand, which in turn . . . and the origin of the original? There you have him.' *The entry on 'foaf' continues* . . . 'An acronym formed from "friend of a friend", that legendary person to whom amazing things allegedly happen. This word was introduced in 1978 by Rodney Dale in his book *The Tumour in the Whale*, a collection of modem urban legends. Initially it was adopted by other students of contemporary folklore, who have added the derivatives *foaflore* and *foaftale*; now it is gaining wider currency, although it has yet to appear in any general dictionary.'

Being as I am an addicted acronymist, the word foaf came naturally to me, delightful with its clodhopping connotations. But who was the genius who recognised the homophony between 'foaf' and 'folk' to give us foaftale and foaflore? Not a rhetorical question; does anyone know the answer?

In the same year as the Longman entry (1990) the *Concise Oxford Dictionary* gives: '**legend** an inauthentic story popularly regarded as true', as does the *New SOD*, adding that this meaning dates from the middle of the nineteenth century (*ie* 1830–69).

As for the new series of my favourite *Collins Dictionary*, there is no enlightenment in the first two editions; the 3rd edition (1994) gives: '**urban legend** a story, especially one with a shocking or amusing ending, related as having actually happened, usually to someone vaguely connected to the teller.' The 4th & 5th editions (1998 & 2000) give the same definition, but extend the headwords from '**urban legend**' to '**urban myth or legend**'.

NOD of 1998 gives '**urban myth** (also chiefly in US **urban legend**) > *noun* an entertaining story or piece of information, circulated as though true, especially one purporting to involve someone vaguely related or known to the teller.'

The *New Penguin English Dictionary* of 2000 gives '**urban legend** *noun* = URBAN MYTH' and then '**urban myth** *noun* a usually amusing, bizarre or horrific tale, in general circulation, that is alleged to be the personal experience of somebody indirectly related to or acquainted with the teller.'

There is, of course, a necessary time-lag between the emergence of a new word or meaning, and a lexicographer (1) hearing of it, (2) deciding that it's here to stay, and (3) having a dictionary on the stocks in which to publish it. We can but wait.

Well, at last *Polyphemus* has arrived at Dawlish, Arthur and Tom have shut the old girl down on a siding and gone for docky, and we can move from the general forest to fresh woods and inspect the individual trees. Thank you.

Bibliography

ACKERMANN, A. *Popular fallacies explained and corrected*. London, 1924.

ASH, Russell *Fact or fiction? A dossier on old beliefs that die hard*. London, 1973.

ASIMOV, Isaac. 'Jokester' in *Earth is room enough*. London, 1960.

BELLOC-LOWNDES, Mrs [Marie Adelaide]. *The end of her honeymoon*. London, 1913

BETT, Henry. *English Myths and traditions*. London, 1952.

The HOLY BIBLE: Apocrypha. *Bel and the dragon*.

BONAPARTE, Marie [Princess George of Greece]. *Myths of war* (Trans J Rodker). London, 1947.

BOOKER, Christopher. *The seven basic plots*. London, 2004.

BREWER, The Rev Dr. *Dr Brewer's guide to science: A guide to the scientific knowledge of things familiar*. London 1865.

BRIGGS, Katharine M. *A dictionary of British folk-tales in the English language including the F J Norton collection*. 4 Vols. London, 1970–1.

BRIGGS, Katharine M and R L Tongue (Eds). *Folktales of England*. With a foreword by R M Dorson. London, 1969.

BRUNVAND, Jan Harold.

The vanishing hitchhiker. Toronto, 1981.

The choking doberman & other "new" urban legends. 1984.

The Mexican Pet: More "New" Urban Legends & Some Old Favorites. 1986.

Curses! Broiled Again! The Hottest Urban Legends Going. 1989.

The Baby Train: and Other Lusty Urban Legends. 1993.

American Folklore: An Encyclopedia. 1996.

The Study of American Folklore. 4th edn. 1998.

Too Good to be True: The Colossal Book of Urban Legends. 1999.

The Truth Never Stands in the Way of a Good Story. 2000.

BUCKLAND, Frank. *Curiosities of natural history*.

BULLEN, Frank T. *Creatures of the sea*. Being the life stories of some sea birds, beasts and fishes. London, 1904.

The cruise of the 'Cachalot'. Round the World after sperm whales. London, 1898.

BURLAND, Cottie Arthur. *Myths of life and death*. London, 1974

BURTON, Maurice, and Robert Burton. *Inside the Animal World*. London, 1977.

CAMPBELL, Joseph. *Myths to live by*. London, 1973.

Cassell's book of humorous quotations. Selected and arranged by A K Adams. London, 1969.

CAWTHORNE, Nigel. *The Strange Laws of Old England*. London, 2004.

CHARLES, Robert H (Trans). *The Book of Jubilees*. London, 1917

CHESTERTON, Gilbert K. 'The Blue Cross' in *The innocence of Father Brown*. London, 1916.

COLES, Manning (Pseud = Adelaide F O Manning + M Coles). *Pray Silence*. London, 1940.

CONSTABLE, Ronnie in *Equipment design for the catering industry*. Ed George Glew. London, 1977.

CRESSY, Edward. *Discoveries and inventions of the Twentieth Century*. London, 1930.

DALE, Rodney A M.
  Louis Wain: The man who drew cats. London, 1968; 1991.
  The Tumour in the Whale. London 1978.
  It's True – it happened to a friend. London, 1984.
  About Time a work of fiction. Haddenham, Cambs, 1995.
  Halcyon Days – Recollections of Post-war Vintage Motoring. Haddenham, 1999.
  with George T Sassoon. *The Manna Machine*. London 1978
  with Joan Gray. *Edwardian Inventions*. London 1979

DALI, Salvador. *The secret life of Salvador Dali*. Trans Haakon M. Chevalier. London, 1968.

DAWE, Clyde J. *Tumours in Aquatic Mammals*. London, 1976.

DICKENS, Charles. *Bleak House*. London, 1852.

Dictionary of National Biography. London, 1885; Oxford 2004.

EARL, L A. *Speeding north with the 'Royal Scot'*. A day in the life of a locomotive man. London, 1939.

EMRICH, Duncan. *Folklore on the American land*. Boston [Mass], 1972.

ERNSTING, Walter. *The day the gods died*. Trans Wendayne Ackerman. London, 1977.

EVANS, Bergen.
  The natural history of nonsense. London, 1947.
  The spoor of spooks. London, 1955.

EYRE-TODD, George (Trans) *The Bruce.* Being the metrical history of Robert the Bruce, King of Scots, compiled AD 1375 by John Barbour. London, 1907.

FURNISS, Harry. *Confessions of a caricaturist.* 2 Vols London, 1901.

GARFIELD, Sydney. *Teeth, teeth, teeth.* London, 1972.

GLAISTER, J. *Medical jurisprudence and toxicology.* Eds. Edgar Rentoul and Hamilton Smith, 13th edn. London, 1973.

GOULD, George M and Walter L Pyle. *Anomalies and curiosities of medicine.* Philadelphia, 1897.

GRUNDY. *Punch*, 8 June (p106) and 29 June (p232). London, 1977.

Guinness book of records. Ed Norris McWhirter, 23rd edn. London, 1976.

HAMILTON, Bethany. *Soul-Surfer.* New York, 2004.

HAMMERTON, Sir John A. *As the days go by: Leaves from my war diary 1939–40.* London, 1941.

HARRISON, Michael. *Fire from heaven.* London, 1976.

HAWKINS, Gerald S. *Stonehenge decoded.* London, 1970.

HEALY, Phil and Rick Glanvill.
 Urban Myths. London, 1992.
 The Return of Urban Myths. London 1993.
 Urban Myths Unplugged. London 1994.

HEIM, Alice W.
 'An experiment on humour'. *Brit. J. Psych*, Vol 27, pp141–61. 1936.
 Intelligence and personality. London, 1970.

HERSEY, John. *Hiroshima.* London, 1946.

HOFFNUNG, Gerard. *Hoffnung at the Oxford Union: The Bricklayer.* Decca record DFE 8682. 1958.

HOGG, Ian & John Weeks. *Military small-arms of the twentieth century,* 2nd edn. London, 1973.

JEFFREYS, D. *Aspirin – The Remarkable Story of a Wonder Drug.* London, 2004.

JONES, Professor R V. *Most secret war.* London, 1977; 1999.

LEE, Ken. *Happy as a sandbag*: A musical.

LEGMAN, G. *The rationale of the dirty joke.* 2 Vols. London, 1972.

LE POER TRENCH, William Francis Brinsly. *Secret of the ages.* UFOs from inside the earth. London, 1974.

LIEPMAN, Heinz. *Rasputin – a new judgment.* Trans Edward Fitzgerald. London. 1959.

MACKAY, Alan (Ed). *The harvest of a quiet eye*. A selection of scientific quotations London, 1977.

MARRYAT, Capt Frederick. *Jacob Faithful*. London, 1834.

MAYHEW, Henry. *Mayhew's London*. Ed. Peter Quennell. London, 1959.

MELLY, George. *Owning up*. London, 1965; 2000.

MILES John A. 'Laughing at the Bible: Jonah as a parody'. *Jewish Quarterly Review*. January 1975.

MINNEY, Rubeigh James, *Rasputin*. London, 1972.

Lord MONTAGU of Beaulieu. *The gilt and the gingerbread*. London, 1967.

MORRIS, Simon. 'Hot rats'. *Oz*, No. 44. September, 1972.

MUGGERIDGE, Malcolm and Hugh KINGSMILL. *Brave old world*. London, 1936.

MULLEN, Revd Peter. Letter to the *Sunday Telegraph* 9 April 2000.

MUNCHAUSEN, Baron (Pseud). *The travels and surprising adventures of Baron Munchausen*.

PARASCIENCE: feature in *New Scientist*, Vol 75, No 1060 pp74–83. 14 July 1977.

PARSONS, Denys. *All too true*. London, 1954.

PARTRIDGE, Eric. *The shaggy dog story: its origin, development and nature*, London, 1954.

POE, Edgar Allan. *The popular tales of Edgar Allan Poe*.

POPE-HENNESSY, James. *Queen Mary 1867–1953*. London, 1959.

PORTER, Enid M. *Cambridgeshire customs and folklore*. London, 1969.

POTTER, Stephen. *Lifemanship*, London, 1950, 1952.

PROTHEROE, Ernest. *Handy natural history of mammals*. London, 1909.

PUNCH Vol 56, p96. London, 1869.

RADZINSKY, Edward. *Rasputin: the last word*. London, 2000.

RATTIGAN, Terence. *Flare Path*.

REYNOLDS, Stanley. 'When the Southland gave birth to the blues' *Radio Times*. 13–19 November 1976.

RIPLEY, Robert L.
    The Omnibus Believe it or Not. London, 1956.
    The Mammoth Believe it or Not. London, 1956.

RISING, Lawrence, *She who was Helen Cass*.

ROACH, Mary. *Stiff*. London, 2003.

SANDERS, Dierdre *et al*. *Would you believe it?* London, 1973–78

SASSOON, George & Rodney A M Dale. *The Manna Machine*. London. 1979.

SEABROOK, Jeremy 'A change in atmosphere: race in one town'. *New Society*, Vol 37, pp 486–91. 2 September 1976.

SHARP, Gerald. *The siege of Ladysmith*. London 1976.

SHAW, George Bernard. *Androcles and the Lion*.

SKRABANEK, Petr & James McCormick *Follies and Fallacies in Medicine*. Glasgow, 1989.

SMITH, H Allen. *The compleat practical joker*. London 1954.

SPERLING, Harry and Maurice Simon (Trans). *The Zohar*, 5 Vols. London, 1931–4.

SQUIERS, Granville. *Secret hiding places*. London, 1933.

SUTHERLAND James (Ed). *The Oxford book of literary anecdotes*. Oxford, 1975.

SYMONS, Julian G. *Buller's campaign*. London, 1963.

THOMPSON, Stith. *Motif-index of folk-literature*. 6 Vols. Copenhagen, 1955.

TRACHTENBERG, Joshua. *The devil and the Jews*. New Haven, 1945.

TURNER, Ernest S. *The phoney war on the home front*. London, 1961.

WALTERS, Cumine (Ed). *Bygone Suffolk*. London, 1901.

WATSON, Lyall. *The Romeo error*. London, 1974.

WAY, R. *Antique dealer*. London, 1957.

WIGRAM, George V. *Englishman's Hebrew and Chaldee concordance to the Old Testament*. London, 1860.

WILSON, Colin. *Rasputin and the fall of the Romanovs*. London, 1964.

WOOD, Revd J G. *The Popular Natural History*. London, 1886.

WOOLLCOTT, Alexander. *While Rome burns*. London, 1934.

WARD, Philip. *A dictionary of common fallacies*. Cambridge, 1978.

WATSON, Revd John Selby. *Reasoning power in animals*. London, 1867.

Website: www.snopes.com *et al*.

Index